ILLICIT DRUG USE IN PORTSMOUTH AND HAVANT

ILLICIT DRUG USE IN PORTSMOUTH AND HAVANT

A local study of a national problem

COLIN BROWN and JEAN LAWTON

Policy Studies Institute

PSI Publications are obtainable from all good bookshops, or by visiting the Institute at: 100 Park Village East, London NW1 3SR (01-387 2171).

Sales Representation: Pinter Publishers Ltd.

Individual and Bookshop orders to: Marston Book Services Ltd, P.O. Box 87, Oxford, OX4 1LB.

A CIP catalogue recor[illegible] this book [illegible] available from the British Library.

PSI Research Report 674

ISBN 0 85374 341 X

Laserset by Policy Studies Institute

Printed by Bourne Offset Ltd, Iver, Bucks.

CONTENTS

TABLES

Notes

(1) For most of the tables, percentages are rounded to the nearest whole number.

(2) A dash (-) denotes zero; asterisk (*) denotes a percentage greater than zero but smaller than 0.5; 'na' denotes data not available.

PREFACE

In 1985 a committee of representatives from different services working in the field of illicit drugs met to consider the extent of the problem in the Portsmouth and Havant area, and in Hampshire as a whole. They soon agreed the need for a project to collate the available facts and figures and to conduct fresh research on the local drugs scene. The Policy Studies Institute was invited to carry out the work, and the research began in 1986. This is the report of the study, published in the same form as it was presented to the committee.

The committee, titled the Research Steering Group, has met regularly throughout the project and given advice and assistance to the researchers. The following people have been members of the Group at different times:

Mr D Basson (Hampshire Constabulary)
Mr P Blaker (Hampshire Constabulary)
Mr J East (Hampshire Social Services)
Dr P Fleming (Wessex Regional Drug Dependency Services)
Mr J Hoddinott (Hampshire Constabulary)
Mr J Holland (Hampshire Probation Service)
Mr R Humphries (Hampshire Social Services) (Chairman of Steering Group)
Ms J Isaacs (Hampshire Health Education)
Mr M Morgan (Hampshire Health Education)
Mr D Noble (Hampshire Constabulary)
Mr D Salmon (Hampshire Constabulary)
Dr S Sheikh (Northern Road Drug Advice Centre; Portsmouth Department of Community Medicine)
Mr D Ward (Hampshire Social Services)

The project was funded by the following bodies: the Wessex Regional Health Authority, the Portsmouth and South East Hampshire Health Authority, the Hampshire Police Authority, Hampshire Social Services, the Hampshire Joint Finance Pool and the Police Foundation. The schools survey was conducted jointly with Portsmouth and South East Hampshire Health Education Unit, which also provided part of the funding for that section of the work. The pooling of the resources of so many organisations is an example of the potential effectiveness of inter-agency co-operation over the problems of drug abuse.

We are also grateful to the Joseph Rowntree Memorial Trust for providing funding for PSI's background research into the drugs problem and into the methodology of fieldwork among drug users; without that work the research described in this report would not have been possible.

We were helped by many people during our research, and we are unable to mention them all here. The busy staff of the social services and the probation service gave us a lot of information. The police were very helpful, although it should be noted that no information about drug users was passed back to them. The staff of the Northern Road Centre were especially helpful and encouraging.

Jane Isaacs deserves our special thanks for the contribution she made to the design and planning of the schools survey. We are also grateful to the officers of the Portsmouth and South East Hampshire Areas of the Hampshire Education Authority for their help; in particular, Howard Probert and Peter Gilliat assisted us greatly in the administration of the survey. Our thanks also go to the head teachers and staff of the schools and colleges for their co-operation and interest.

Most of all our thanks go to the people we can never name: the drug users who talked with us and helped us in many ways with the research. We are grateful for their trust and friendliness. Our hope is that the project will contribute to the improvement of local services for local people with drug problems.

1 INTRODUCTION

For several years now the headlines about illicit drugs have been demanding the attention of everyone who cares about their community. There has been no shortage of stories to feed the nightmares of parents worried about their sons and daughters: newspapers and TV documentaries have been crowded with images of teenagers lost to a sordid life of addiction, crime and illness. Advertisements and leaflets produced by the government have reinforced these images, and statements by politicians and other public figures have drawn attention to the increase in drug abuse and its dangers. Faced with these alarms, people are rightly concerned to know the facts about the drugs threat to young people. What is the problem and how bad is it? Who is involved? Is there a drugs epidemic?

This report gives the results of a research project on the extent and nature of illicit drug use in a specific geographical area: Portsmouth and Havant. It is based on the collection of information from local sources and on two social surveys, one of school pupils and the other of local drug users. The emphasis of the report is on facts and figures, and on what has happened up to now, rather than on speculation and on what might happen in the future. This makes for duller stuff than some of the other coverage of the subject, but the intention here is to provide a clear picture of what is happening in the area studied.

Although this is a local study, it is concerned with issues of national importance. Research on this scale is relevant to the wider issues for three reasons. First, the drugs problem is not uniform throughout Britain, but is made up of differing local patterns, and information on the conditions in the various parts of the country is important for understanding what is happening nationally. Secondly, a local perspective is needed to illustrate the social aspects of the problem. National statistics can give the impression that illicit drug users are isolated individuals, but the reality is one of intricate relationships, and local studies are able to focus on the 'drug scene' and its social dynamics. The can also touch other aspects of the users' social world, and give some clues about their motivations. Thirdly, a local study can give attention to the way services respond, and relate that to the experience of drug users; this is relevant to national concerns over ways of helping users give up and preventing others from starting.

The growth of the problem nationally

In addition to the alarming reports from parts of the country where there are particular problems, there are some facts which clearly indicate a general growth of illicit drug use in Britain. The last decade has seen a rise in the numbers of notified addicts, seizures of drugs by the police and customs, and proceedings against people for drug offences. Some of the figures are examined more closely later in the report, but a brief account here will show the extent of the changes.

The number of narcotic drug addicts notified by doctors to the Home Office is an imperfect measure of the extent of addiction, but it shows an unmistakeable upward trend in the use of opiates. During the whole of 1979 just under 4,500 addicts were notified in England, but by 1985 this had risen to 13,000. The number of new addicts notified per year rose over the same period from just under 1,500 to just over 5,500. Together these indicators show a roughly threefold increase in the visible extent of addiction over six years. Seizures of heroin by the police in the UK show an even steeper rise from about 600 in 1980 to about 3,000 in 1985. Over the same period there was also a steep rise in the seizures of amphetamine (645 to 3,245). There were also increases, though less dramatic ones, for cannabis resin (6,216 to 13,732), cocaine (365 to 509), and LSD (243 to 448). Thus, although these figures indicate an increase in the use of illicit drugs generally, it is the use of opiates that seems to have escalated most alarmingly.

The drugs

Those unfamiliar with the subject tend to lump all illicit drugs together. But the substances covered by the term vary enormously in origins, physical and psychological effects, potency, cost, methods of use, health risks, and the seriousness with which the law views them. No serious attempt to understand illegal drug taking can avoid looking at what the actual drugs are. In the body of this report, it will emerge that some drugs are used by many more people than others, and the nature of the various drugs is of great importance for interpreting the patterns of use. The descriptions below give enough information to make the basic distinctions. For those who wish to read more detailed accounts, Andrew Tyler's paperback 'Street Drugs' is an excellent source of reference and good sense.

Cannabis

This is a term used to describe the substances prepared from the plant Cannabis sativa. Their main active ingredient is tetrahydrocannabinol, known as THC. Many different preparations come from the plant: the gluey resin which is collected from the tops of the female plants is compacted into bars, while parts of the plant itself are cut, dried and bundled up in varying forms. Both the resin and the herbal drug come in different qualities, and are sometimes adulterated by other substances. Most people use cannabis by smoking it mixed with tobacco (although cannabis smoke can be inhaled on its own), but sometimes it is eaten. In the Hampshire area the most common term for cannabis is 'blow'. It gives a general feeling of pleasurable intoxication, but users find the specific effects hard to describe. Sensations also vary considerably from person to person, and between occasions.

Amphetamine

Amphetamine is a stimulant. It is a synthetic drug, and is produced legally and illegally in many different forms. Amphetamine has been produced in tablet form by the pharmaceutical industry under the names Benzedrine, Dexedrine, Durophet, Drinamyl (the famous 'purple hearts' of the 1960s), Pemoline, Ritalin and Tenuate Dospan; some of these drugs are in fact chemical mimics of amphetamine itself. Illicitly produced amphetamine sulphate comes as a powder, which is sniffed or injected in aqueous solution. The amphetamine is sold to the user mixed with other powders to increase its bulk.

The effects are summed up well by its street names 'speed' and 'whiz': the user feels a general increase in the energy resources of the body and the mind, and personal confidence increases. The user pays for all this later, when the effects wear off: tiredness and depression set in, with a depth that mirrors the earlier high.

Heroin

Heroin is a derivative of opium. The seed pods of the poppy Papaver somniferum yield a liquid which is dried and processed to give opium, and further extensive chemical treatment produces heroin. It is pharmaceutically produced in various forms for oral and intravenous administration. Illicitly produced heroin usually appears as a powder, again mixed with other powders by the time it reaches the streets. It is ingested by smoking, sniffing or by injecting it dissolved in water. It is usually called 'smack' by local users.

The main effects are analgesia and sedation. Physical pain is reduced, and so is mental pain: the user's awareness of the troubles of life is replaced by a warm, dozy satisfaction.

Other opiates

Heroin is not the only opium derivative. Several others are available on prescription or illicitly: morphine, a pharmaceutical product which pre-dates heroin; codeine, a familiar pain-killer which is considerably less powerful than heroin and morphine, but is nevertheless a narcotic; and opium itself, the illicit form of which is generally smoked.

Synthetic drugs which act like opiates are called opioids. The most important opioid used in the treatment of drug abuse is methadone (Physeptone, known on the street as 'Phy'): it is the main drug prescribed as a substitute for heroin when users are trying to bring their habit under control, or to an end. It is most commonly provided in a green mixture to be swallowed (the mixture cannot be injected). Dipipanone is another opioid, and is the main active ingredient of Diconal tablets. These tablets are intended for oral use as an analgesic, but some people grind them up and mix them with water for injection. A weaker opioid called dihydrocodeine is contained in DF-118 tablets. There are other opioids, but the only one that shows up with any frequency on the illicit drug market is dextromoramide (Palfium). For the sake of simplicity, the term 'opiates' used in the rest of this report also embraces the opioids.

Cocaine

Cocaine ('coke') is a stimulant that is refined from the leaves of the Latin American coca plant. Most of the cocaine in the UK is cocaine hydrochloride, a white powder which, like the other powdered drugs, arrives on the street mixed with other things. It is usually sniffed, but sometimes users dissolve it in water and use a syringe. Another refined form is the more potent freebase cocaine, known also as 'crack', which comes in the form of small lumps, and is smoked.

The effect of cocaine is like a high-class version of amphetamine: it is said to be smoother and more enjoyable, although the duration of effect is much shorter than with amphetamine. It is also a local anaesthetic. Freebase cocaine has a more immediate and stronger effect, but this is very short-lived and leaves the user craving for another smoke.

LSD and 'magic mushrooms'

LSD (d-lysergic acid diethylamide, known more commonly as 'acid') is a hallucinogenic drug derived chemically from a fungus called ergot. It is produced in liquid form, then dried on paper; squares of the paper are sold and taken orally. It has turned up in other forms, for example as small tablets and on sugar lumps. The Liberty Cap mushroom (Psilocybe semilanceata) contains a similar drug. More rarely used is the Fly Agaric mushroom (Amanita muscaria).

LSD is a powerful mind-altering drug that warps the user's perceptions and induces hallucinations. Users say that it can be a profound experience as well as an exciting one, but the wrong mood or the wrong environment can produce a 'bad trip' of terrifying visions and paranoia. The mushrooms produce different hallucinogenic experiences. According to Tyler, the Liberty Cap produces a smoother, calmer trip than LSD, while the effects of the Fly Agaric are more tangible physically, and are more uncomfortable.

There are other hallucinogenic drugs but they are rare in this country: mescaline, PCP ('angel dust') and MDMA ('ecstacsy') are relatively well-known in the USA.

Barbiturates and benzodiazepines

Barbiturates are synthetic hypnosedatives ('downers' to drug users) produced by the pharmaceutical industry, generally as tablets and capsules: Tuinal, Nembutal and Seconal are common ones. Their effects are to calm people down, and at higher dosages to knock them out or cause erratic, drunken behaviour.

Benzodiazepines are tranquillisers: the most famous brand names are Librium (chlordiazepoxide) and Valium (diazepam), but there are many others, and they are prescribed in large numbers in tablet form. Their effects are calming and, at higher dosages, stupefying and sleep-inducing.

Volatile inhalants

Many household and industrial products contain volatile solvents which cause intoxication when their vapour is inhaled. Glue-sniffing is only the best-known version. The effect is much like drunkenness, but sniffers can also experience hallucinations.

Amyl nitrite and butyl nitrite, first used medically for easing angina pains, are commercially produced liquids whose vapour is inhaled to produce a giddy rush of excitement. They are not controlled drugs.

The research project

Three separate elements comprise the project: the prevalence study, the survey of young people in schools and colleges, and the interview survey of drug users. The chapters of this report deal with each in turn.

The prevalence study was made up of several elements: first a round of interviews with people working in local agencies having some dealings with illicit drug users; second, a collation of available statistics on the use of illicit drugs, locally and in the county; and third, a systematic review of the case-loads of the main agencies dealing with drug users. The prevalence study was based partly on the methods described in the guide produced by the Drug Indicators Project at Birkbeck College.

The survey of young people was a survey of 1,063 pupils and students in schools and further education colleges. Its aim was to gather information on the leisure patterns and life-styles of young people aged between 11 and 19, and to relate that to their use of alcohol, tobacco and illicit drugs.

The survey of drug users involved 41 interviews with people who used illicit drugs. It was aimed at opiate users in particular. The interviews were wide-ranging, and covered their history of drug abuse, their domestic circumstances, housing, employment, family history, health and diet, and views about drugs and drug-taking. We have tried to avoid presenting the results in a lurid way: sometimes people report the more exciting (and gruesome) material from interviews of this kind with too much relish, and that only adds to the distorted image of the drugs problem which is the source of so much worry.

By combining information from a variety of sources in a single study we hope to overcome some of the difficulties inherent in research on activities that are illegal and subject to social disapproval. Most of these activities are hidden from view and are inaccessible to routine official data collection, and the picture has to be built up from fragments obtained in a number of different ways, including the admissions of people involved. None of the sources of data used in this study would on its own give a reliable account of the scale and nature of the drugs problems in Portsmouth and Havant, but by testing one against another and combining them we reach a much better overview.

The main focus of the study is on illegal drugs, and for the most part it avoids the subject of legal drug abuse. The problems associated with tobacco, alcohol and prescribed tranquillisers are enormous, and in health terms alone are on a far greater scale than the problems of illegal drugs. The very size of the legal drug problem is the main reason why we could not include it: it would have swamped the rest of the project. Although we have concentrated on the use of illicit drugs, we have tried not to treat it as a problem that is isolated from other drug use. Particular attention is given to the links between licit and illicit drugs in the discussions of the schools survey and the drug user interviews.

The geographical area of the study

The study looks at the use of illicit drugs within Hampshire. In particular, the three main elements of the project are concentrated on the area within the local authority boundaries of Portsmouth and Havant, situated in the south-east of the county. The map shows the extent of the boundaries. The population of the two local authorities together is over 300,000 and accounts for a fifth of the total population of Hampshire. Although Havant covers geographical area one-and-a-half times the size of Portsmouth, its population is the smaller of the two: Havant has just under 120,000 residents and Portsmouth has just under 190,000.

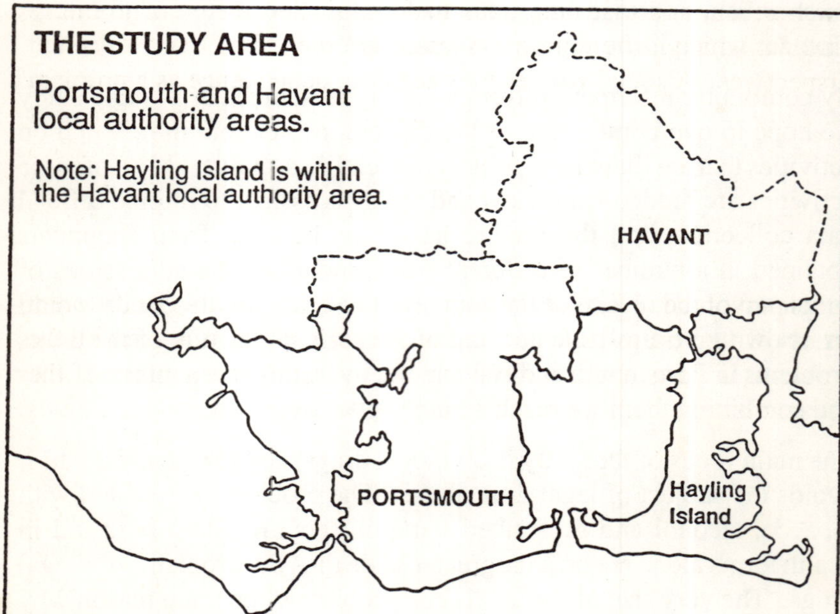

2 ESTIMATING THE EXTENT OF LOCAL DRUG ABUSE

One of the project's tasks was to assess the scale of the illicit drugs problem in the Portsmouth and Havant area. The drugs problem, however, is not a single thing: it is made up of many different problems to do with many different drugs, which are seen from many different perspectives. A social worker may see drug dependence as a problem because it can wreck the lives of vulnerable people; a police officer may see illicit drug use as a problem because it is illegal and sometimes leads to other crimes; a drug user may see drugs as a problem because they are expensive. None of them is likely to see cannabis in the same light as heroin, but they are unlikely to agree about the difference.

In this part of the report we try to do two things: to unpick the different strands of 'the drugs problem' in the area, mainly as it is seen by the professionals, and to give some idea of the numbers of users of the different drugs. The information comes from four sources: discussions with those who came into contact with the drugs problem in the course of their work, interviews with drug users, the collection and collation of the factual information and statistics relating to drug abuse, and a survey of young people in schools and colleges. Most of the detailed findings of the interviews with users and the survey of young people are presented in later sections of the report, but some of the relevant material is presented here.

Drug abuse in Portsmouth and Havant - the agencies

A variety of bodies deal with illicit drug use, their functions ranging from therapeutic and educational work to law enforcement. Some are concerned specifically with drug abuse, while others come into contact with users as part of a much wider job.

The Northern Road Drug Advice Centre in Cosham is at the heart of the area's services both for helping drug users and for drug education and advice. Their work has been documented in detail in a recent report by Portsmouth Polytechnic's Social Services Research and Information Unit. Northern Road runs as a drop-in advice centre for users and others concerned about drugs. It has a staff of doctors, community psychiatric nurses, a social worker, administrative support workers and volunteers. It has a case-load of drug users who have sought help, and much of the activity of the staff is around these people, both at the Centre and on home visits. Although a large number of the clients have a history of heroin use, the centre is open to anyone who has a problem with any drug, and a substantial minority of clients have a problem with prescribed tranquillisers. The service provided by NRC is confidential - users can phone the centre or pay a visit in the knowledge that the information will not be passed to the police. The staff run drop-in sessions at health centres and probation centres, and are involved with educational and advice work in schools and other local groups.

Connected with the Northern Road Centre is the detoxification unit, situated during this study at St James' Hospital in Milton. The eleven-bed unit, Highclere, provided a place for users to spend the early period of coming off drugs under medical supervision. Since the completion of this study the unit has been moved to the same site as the Northern Road Centre.

Drug users also come into contact with the medical services through their general practitioners and through the accident and emergency services. GPs are sometimes approached for help in coming off, but are also approached as potential sources of supply. The range of opiates that doctors can normally supply is limited, but users are sometimes able to support part of a habit from prescriptions obtained from GPs, either legitimately or under false pretences. Chemists, of course, come into contact with all of the users who are taking prescribed drugs.

Outside the immediate area there are several residential facilities for people who want to give up illicit drugs, to which Northern Road clients are sometimes referred. The most important of them is Alpha House at Droxford, which also has a 'half-way house' in Southsea where ex-users can begin to rebuild their lives in the community.

The probation service has a substantial number of drug users among its clients. Many of these people have been convicted either of actual drug offences or of offences committed to fund an expensive drug habit. The social services also see drug users, but fewer of them. This is for two reasons. First, a large proportion of illicit drug users are young, single, able-bodied adults - a section of the population that the social services do not have a lot to do with; secondly, drug users who are clients of the social services will often have very good reasons to conceal their habit - for example, parents of young children may fear that they will be taken into care. At a county level, Hampshire Social Services have a specialist drugs adviser, stationed at Northern Road Centre.

The police have contact with the illicit drugs world in two ways: in the course of day-to-day police work, and through the work of the drugs squads and the regional crime squad. Part of the reason for their contact is the illegality of the whole business, from supply to possession and consumption, but it is also a result of the involvement of a significant number of illicit drug users in non-drug crimes.

On the educational front, there is a drugs education specialist employed at county level who works with local health education officers to provide training for teachers and others, the aim being that the health education effort among young people should mainly be carried out by teachers and others who already work with children, rather than by professional drugs educators. The Royal Navy has a drugs education service based in Portsmouth, and its officers lecture and show films to recruits and to other groups of young people with naval connections.

There are many other professionals who have contacts with drug users in this area, but those listed above are the main ones. In addition, there are enthusiastic voluntary workers involved. There are branches of Families Anonymous and Narcotics Anonymous in the area.

Many of the organisations mentioned above come together under the umbrella of the District Drugs Advisory Committee, which meets every two months. This acts partly as a co-ordinating body and as a forum for exchange of information and ideas among those working in the drugs field.

In a list of facilities and services for drug abusers, their sources of supply ought to be mentioned. As we have already noted, some users obtain drugs from chemists: some obtain prescriptions for opiates, opioids, tranquillisers or amphetamines from GPs; oral methadone is supplied to some of the Northern Road Centre's clients, some on a basis of gradual reduction leading to withdrawal, but others on a basis of maintenance; and sometimes drugs are obtained illegally, either by forged prescriptions, or by break-ins. Most of the drugs, however, are bought on the black market. There are several pubs and clubs in the area that are well known among users as places to contact others and to arrange the purchase of drugs. For obvious reasons, those involved are elusive and secretive, and there are other problems when trying to build up a picture of the local drugs supply. The commercial structure of the illicit drug market is complicated, the most confusing element being the impossibility of drawing a firm line between the suppliers and the supplied.

The professionals' assessments

We spoke to people from all the organisations mentioned and came away with many different accounts of 'the facts'. Many people were conscious that their view was a partial one, but a few were convinced that their version was the correct one and that others saw things in a distorted way.

There are some items of consensus. Everyone we spoke to agreed that the use of cannabis was now widespread. They also agreed that the use of cocaine was very limited, despite the nightmarish headline prophesies about the plans of American exporters to flood the European drug market. Most agreed that the use of heroin had increased over the past five years, but there was dispute about the extent of that growth. All the professionals who had been in the area long enough said that the local drugs scene had existed for many years and some of its features are perennial. The popularity of amphetamines, both as powder and pills, is not new, and, although it is not on a par with cannabis, it is certainly the next most widespread illicit drug. There were frequent mentions of the availability of LSD, although it was felt that few people used it regularly; the proximity of the countryside means that it is also possible to gather 'magic mushrooms' and their use was mentioned by many people.

The strongest agreement was over the seriousness of the problems caused by legal drugs: tranquillisers and alcohol. Most agreed that the excessive use of prescribed tranquillisers, particularly by women, amounted to a drug problem in its own right. But the most alarming comments were reserved for the abuse of alcohol: everyone agreed that it caused problems on a far greater scale than those caused by other drugs. This is particularly true for violence on the street and in the home: it should be noted that the violence that so often accompanies alcohol abuse is rarely seen as a result of illicit drug use. Apart from the Northern Road Centre and the drugs squad, all of the agencies we spoke to spent much more time dealing with drink than with drugs.

Those interviewed in the social services said they had few contacts with drug users, and therefore they mainly had indirect information. They felt that the problem was patchy, and was often overstated; two people at a senior level said that if anything the problem in their areas had eased recently, but in another area the picture was one of increasing heroin use. The social services had no children in care as a result of problems with illicit drugs, although there were some parents known to have a habit. Cases of young glue sniffers did come to the notice of social workers, but it was difficult to tell whether the problem was getting worse or not.

The probation service sees a lot of drug users, but they are the ones who have been caught, and inevitably among them the more 'serious' users (or, perhaps, those who used to be more serious) are over-represented, so they give a biased impression of the drugs scene. Even so, the most common drugs mentioned are alcohol, cannabis and amphetamine, in that order. It was said to us that the Portsmouth drugs scene declined after a number of arrests of dealers in the late 1970s, but was now building up again.

Those working with young people outside schools said they knew of little heroin use but saw a disturbing amount of drunkenness. Like the social workers, they commented on the way that drug use was very patchy, and that different drugs appeared then disappeared in different localities. In some areas, for example, cannabis was becoming fashionable among youngsters while solvent abuse was declining. They emphasised the fact that amphetamines had always been popular with some groups aged between 18 and 25. They also mentioned the use of amyl nitrite ('poppers') by teenagers at discos and clubs; amyl nitrite is not illegal and can be bought over the counter.

The staff at the Northern Road Centre have a well-formed picture of the drugs scene, although it is naturally influenced by the particular characteristics of their clients, who are often long-term users who have a history of many different drugs. Like others, the staff mentioned the geographical clustering of users. They said that heroin seemed to be on the increase, and so was amphetamine, while there was little evidence of cocaine use. They were concerned about the black market availability of prescribed drugs, which had grown. Particularly worrying was the street sale of Diconal, an opioid which is intended for oral use but which users often attempt to dissolve in water, then inject; used in this way Diconal is a very dangerous drug, but many opiate users like it a lot. The staff said the use of barbiturates had declined over the years, but they are still available on the black market. The Centre had contact with about 130 opiate and opioid users, and worked with the assumption that these represented about a fifth of all the users in the area.

The police also have a lot of information about illicit drugs, although what is collected is influenced by their own objectives of law enforcement, particularly identifying heroin dealers and supply networks. We spoke to officers in the drugs squad and the regional crime squad, and their account of drug availability and use was in essence very similar to that given by the Northern Road staff: widespread cannabis use; increasing availability of heroin and amphetamine; few barbiturates; locally available Diconal; LSD available, but no regular following. The police also mentioned the widespread use of Pemoline, something we heard from no-one else.

Pemoline is a prescribed drug, an amphetamine variant which is a class C drug under the Misuse of Drugs Act, unlike amphetamine itself, which is a class B drug; class C drugs attract lighter penalties.

Voluntary workers

Those working with drug users as part of the voluntary sector tended to have a view of the drugs scene that was more alarming. Qualitatively, their views were not very different from those we have already mentioned, with the exception that there was a greater emphasis on cocaine and its highly addictive variant, crack (there was no other evidence to suggest that any crack had been seen in the area). The main difference was over the scale of the problem. The voluntary workers talked of more widespread use of illicit drugs, and of heroin in particular.

The users' views

We asked a group of illicit drug users for their general impression of the drugs scene and for their estimate of the proportion of opiate users in contact with the Northern Road Centre.

It is interesting to note that they did not always agree with each others' accounts of the size of the local drug scene. This is probably because there is no single drug scene, but a set of them, loosely bound together by common friendships and mutual interests. These groups of people are divided to some extent by the different drugs they use: for example, opiate users form a more closely-knit group than people who use only cannabis. But groups of users are also divided by geography. Where you live determines what you see, and the local variations in drug abuse can produce extraordinary differences in people's perceptions of what is going on in the area as a whole.

Estimates of the number of users of heroin ranged from hundreds to thousands, and estimates of the number of users in contact with Northern Road varied from one per cent to over three-quarters. This variation means that the users' views are not very useful for estimating the scale of local drug use. As regards trends, some users said there was more heroin available now than there had been in the past, but others said that there had always been a big drugs scene; nobody said that heroin availability had declined. Some of the users said that there were more young people involved than there used to be, but more of them commented that, on the contrary, they knew of few teenage heroin users. We came across hardly any teenage users in our own fieldwork, but our contacts were mainly made through older users and this might have limited our opportunities to meet younger ones.

All of the users agreed that there was a very large number of cannabis users in the area. In fact they were often dismissive of cannabis use, as if to say it was not 'proper' drug use; for example, most interpreted our questions on coming off drugs as being about opiates and amphetamines. Several said they thought a majority of the population smoked cannabis, a view which grossly overestimates its use but which illustrates the extent to which users of harder drugs regard cannabis as an everyday drug. Users thought that amphetamines were widely consumed, but not as widely as cannabis. There was a difference between younger and older users in the way they talked about amphetamine. Many experienced drug users regarded it as a serious and unhealthy drug, and some had come to hate it. Less experienced users tended to see it as more benign, and were more casual about it.

The drug market

We were given a good deal of information about the local drug market, although, as we said earlier, it was difficult to obtain firm facts. Since dealing in drugs is illegal, neither researchers nor anyone else can be sure that what they are told is true, regardless of assurances of confidentialtiy. However, the information that we have been given by users fits largely with that given by the police and by other drugs workers, and is not contradicted by any of the recorded drug events, such as seizures, arrests and prescriptions.

One key to understanding the local drugs trade is the ease of communications with London. The A3 provides a two-hour run by car to South London, and the train takes only an hour and a half. Most of the illicit drugs come down from London. Hampshire does not have any large-scale distribution centres, and there seem to be no 'drug barons'. There are instead a fair number of medium and small-time dealers. In addition to the route from London, we were told that some drugs, particularly amphetamines, come from Southampton and further west. Some people have asked us whether Portsmouth is at special risk from illicit drugs because it is a port; the answer seems to be no. If drugs do come in through Portsmouth in quantity, they are on their way to London or further north.

Locally, the distribution network is extremely complicated and seems to change all the time. The problem is that users with an expensive habit often sell drugs at a profit in order to finance their own use, so it is appropriate to talk of user-dealers in addition to users and dealers. Moreover, roles can be reversed with time, so that someone may find themselves selling to someone they once bought from. Most user-dealers handle only small quantities; often those who do develop a larger business just increase their own consumption, ending up with a bigger habit and no more money at the end of it.

Some local dealers go to London several times a week for heroin, and may bring back quite small amounts, perhaps to avoid heavy penalties if caught, but also because some trips are made as soon as enough money is raised in advance from prospective customers. Heroin sold in this area is of low average purity. The content of street heroin varies a great deal, but users are lucky to buy anything that has more than 20 per cent heroin, while in London the purity may be over twice as high. All down the distribution chain, the powder is mixed with other substances to make it go further and increase profits, and this is one reason why many users have taken to smoking rather than injecting over recent years: occasionally the 'cuts' mixed with the heroin and other drugs are very unhealthy - although glucose powder is the most common cut, drugs can turn up with disgusting adulterants such as washing powder and brick dust.

Thefts from chemists' shops, forged prescriptions and the manipulation of GPs provide a supply of various pharmaceutically-produced drugs such as Diconal and amphetamines. This means that part of the local drug market amounts to a sort of swap-shop, with users selling some types of drug to raise money to buy others. Some even sell a portion of their prescribed methadone, but this is not a large part of the illicit market.

It would be wrong to think that all dealers handle a wide range of drugs, but it would also be wrong to think that each drug is handled by a specific group of dealers. The market is much more chaotic than that, with some people selling what they can get, and others specialising in one or two drugs most of the time. The cannabis market is by far the biggest, and there are some dealers who concentrate on it.

All black-market supplies of drugs are subject to shortages and interruptions, although users can often find alternative suppliers because there is no single local distribution network. Even cannabis, the most widely available and most widely used illicit drug, suffers from these supply problems. Generally, however, illicit drugs are available to those who have the right connections, as long as they have the money and as long as they are willing to put a little effort into searching for what they want.

All the evidence we could obtain about cocaine suggests that if drug users can afford it they can get it, but few use it. The price is high, the duration of its effect is short and it is rather similar to amphetamine, so people are reluctant to buy it. In addition, the cocaine available locally tends to be cut with a substantial amount of amphetamine powder, and this deters users from spending large sums on it. There was no evidence at all that 'crack' is used in this area.

Notified users of opiates

Some drug users obtain their supplies legally. Under the provisions of the Misuse of Drugs Act, doctors are expected to notify the Home Office of any patient known to be addicted to an opiate. The Home Office publishes annual figures broken down by Police Authority, and these therefore show the trend in the number of addicts recognised by GPs and by doctors working in treatment centres, both nationally and within Hampshire. In addition, the police carry out regular checks on all chemists within the county and keep a list of the users receiving legal supplies of controlled drugs, and it is therefore possible to produce annual figures, both for the county and for the Portsmouth and Havant area, showing the number of addicts legally supplied with opiates.

These sources do not tell us the total number of opiate users. They refer only to those whose addiction has come to the attention of doctors, and this is a minority. The statistics are also deficient because not all doctors report all the addicts they see. However, the numbers of notified addicts can provide invaluable data about the trends in opiate use.

Notifications by doctors

The analysis of the notifications statistics is a little complicated, but its conclusions are simple. In terms of addicts who come to the notice of doctors, the level of drug addiction in Hampshire has been growing over the last ten years, but the problem is not as serious as it is in England as a whole. Furthermore, the Hampshire problem seems to be less volatile, in that there is a relatively low turnover of notified addicts: each year the proportion of the addicts who are newly notified is lower than it is nationally.

Over a year the total number of addicts notified is greater than the number known on any one day. The list changes during the year: new addicts are added, while old names are removed because contact has been lost with them, or because they are no longer addicted, or for various other reasons. The official statistics are published in a form that acknowledges this flow on to and off the register. The Home Office statistics annually show the total number of addicts receiving narcotic drugs at the turn of the year and the total number of addicts newly notified at any time during the year; the latter total is further broken down into new addicts and previously-known addicts who have re-appeared after a period when they were not notified. From these statistics it is possible to calculate the total number of addicts who were notified during the whole year.

The tables in this report show the whole-year totals, the end-of-year totals and the numbers of new addicts notified, for the years 1979 to 1985. We give the figures for Hampshire, for the surrounding counties and for England as a whole. As well as the raw totals, we present the figures in a way that takes into account the different sizes of those areas, by showing the number of addicts per 100,000 people aged 16 to 39 in the population. This enables us to make a direct comparison between the numbers of addicts reported in Hampshire and in the whole country. The 16 to 39 age group is used in preference to the total population because most addicts are within that age range, and it can therefore be regarded as the 'population at risk'.

Table 2.1 shows the whole-year totals of notified addicts in England, in Hampshire, and in the surrounding Police Authorities, for the years 1979 to 1985. Nationally the total has grown every year, and has grown particularly quickly since 1980, from 4,726 to 13,000 in 1985. In Hampshire the growth has been rapid since 1981, from 110 to 230 in 1985. In the surrounding counties the period has seen a general growth in number of addicts, but the trend varies somewhat between counties. In Sussex, the growth has been larger than elsewhere, from 204 addicts in 1980 to 431 in 1985, while there has been little growth in Wiltshire, and none in Dorset.

Table 2.1 Drug addicts reported to Home Office, whole year totals, 1979-1985

	79	80	81	82	83	84	85
Total Addicts							
Hampshire	114	125	110	130	175	216	230
ENGLAND	4448	4726	5663	7204	9173	11157	13000
Thames Valley	64	91	130	167	191	214	188
Dorset	75	58	59	71	65	73	75
Surrey	54	71	97	126	128	158	208
Sussex	171	204	236	286	330	359	431
Wilts	4	7	11	17	22	33	83
Addicts per 100,000 of population aged 16-39							
Hampshire	22	24	21	25	34	42	44
ENGLAND	28	30	36	45	58	70	82
Dorset	43	33	33	40	37	41	43
Surrey	16	21	29	38	38	47	62
Sussex	43	51	59	72	83	90	108
Wilts	2	4	6	9	12	18	46

The number of addicts per 100,000 people shows that Hampshire and Surrey are similar to England as a whole in terms of trends, and a little below it in terms of the numbers; the numbers are much higher for Sussex, but the upward trend is the same. In Dorset the actual level of notified users per 100,000 is of the same order as in Hampshire, Surrey and England as a whole in recent years, but there is no distinct upward trend. The figures for Wiltshire are very low, but there is a notable upward trend.

The end-of-year totals are shown in Table 2.2 and they are all considerably lower than the whole-year totals. The trends, however, and the variations between the areas are very similar to those described above for the whole-year totals.

Table 2.2 Addicts receiving notifiable drugs as treatment at 31 December, 1979-1985

	79	80	81	82	83	84	85
Total Addicts							
Hampshire	78	77	75	94	125	145	166
ENGLAND	2493	2671	3592	4046	4651	5485	6712
Thames Valley	30	40	74	66	83	76	96
Dorset	37	32	30	42	32	36	43
Surrey	36	44	60	79	79	94	113
Sussex	84	122	170	139	147	188	253
Wilts	2	6	7	8	15	16	11
Addicts per 100,000 of population aged 16-39							
Hampshire	15	15	14	18	24	28	32
ENGLAND	16	17	23	25	29	35	42
Dorset	21	18	17	24	18	20	24
Surrey	11	13	18	24	24	28	34
Sussex	21	31	43	35	37	47	64
Wilts	1	3	4	4	8	9	6

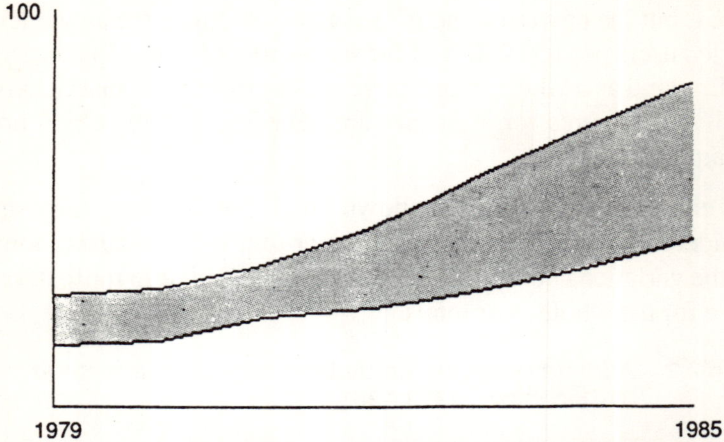

FIGURE 2.1 DRUG ADDICT NOTIFICATIONS IN ENGLAND, 1979-85
Addicts per 100,000 people aged 16-39. Whole year totals (upper line) and end of year total (lower line).

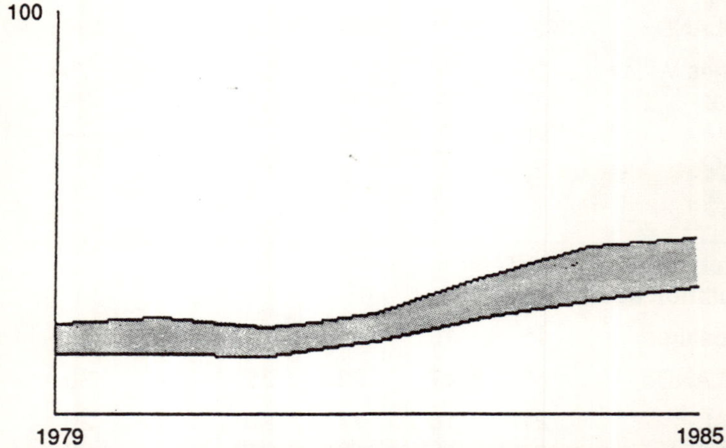

FIGURE 2.2 DRUG ADDICT NOTIFICATIONS IN HAMPSHIRE, 1979-85
Addicts per 100,000 people aged 16-39. Whole year totals (upper line) and end of year total (lower line).

By comparing the whole-year totals and the end-of-year totals, we can see how the turnover of notified addicts is lower in Hampshire than it is nationally. Figures 2.1 and 2.2 show in graphical form the number of addicts per 100,000 people aged 16 to 39. The shaded gap between the lines is made up of users who are known at some point during the year but are not receiving drugs as treatment on one specific day; it is narrower for Hampshire than for England. The turnover is lower in Hampshire for two reasons: first, there are fewer new addicts per year, and second, the known addicts tend to continue being treated, rather than disappearing from the list. In comparison with England as a whole, therefore, Hampshire has a slower growth of reported addiction and a more stable population of medically-supplied addicts.

Table 2.3 New addicts notified to Home Office during year, 1979-1985

	79	80	81	82	83	84	85
Total Addicts							
Hampshire	19	26	15	32	53	63	51
ENGLAND	1454	1454	2015	2418	2631	4740	5511
Thames Valley	30	46	70	61	73	97	82
Dorset	21	14	15	23	17	27	29
Surrey	11	25	30	37	27	61	82
Sussex	51	77	64	76	115	133	165
Wilts	2	3	3	8	7	17	47
Addicts per 100,000 of population aged 16-39							
Hampshire	4	5	3	6	10	12	10
ENGLAND	9	9	13	15	23	30	35
Dorset	12	8	9	13	10	15	16
Surrey	3	7	9	11	8	18	24
Sussex	13	19	16	19	29	33	42
Wilts	1	2	2	4	4	9	26

Table 2.3 gives the actual numbers of new reports of addicts who were not previously known. The national figure has risen a great deal every year since 1980, but the rise in Hampshire has been less steep and less regular. The number of new addicts per 100,000 of the national population at risk grew from 9 to 35 between 1980 and 1985, while in Hampshire the growth was from 5 to 10 over the same period.

Table 2.4 Controlled drugs - chemist notifications, 1978-1987

	78	79	80	81	82	83	84	85	86	87
Total persons notified during year										
(1) Hampshire	56	39	74	71	89	94	159	146	156	170
(2) Portsmouth and Havant	24	16	23	28	35	43	72	68	75	96
(2) as a percentage of (1)	43	41	31	39	39	46	45	47	48	56

Note: 1987 figure covers situation in first half of year.

Prescriptions data

Table 2.4 gives the total number of addicts receiving their supplies by prescription from chemists in Hampshire over the period 1978 to 1987. These figures do not include Hampshire users who get their drugs from chemists outside the county or users who get their drugs direct from treatment centres. They include in some years one or two people habitually using amphetamine tablets, but all the others are opiate users.

The figures for the county follow a trend similar to that of the doctors' notifications, and in fact the numbers are in some years fairly close to the end-of-year totals. They are close enough to allow us to use the prescripions data as a reasonably reliable source of information on the proportion of Hampshire's medically-supplied users living in the Portsmouth and Havant area, and on the trend in the number of such users in the area. The local trend has been upwards since 1979. From 1978 to 1987 the proportion of Hampshire's legally supplied users living in the Portsmouth and Havant area has ranged between 31 and 56 per cent, averaging 43 per cent. Only about 20 per cent of Hampshire's total population lives in the area; this means that there are proportionately twice as many legally supplied users in Portsmouth and Havant as in the rest of the county. The actual number in the study area rose from 16 in 1979 to 70 in 1984, dipped a little to 68 in 1985, then rose again to 96 in 1987. The great majority of them were receiving methadone, supplied as a result of their contact with the Northern Road Centre.

The sharpest local increase was between 1986 and 1987, from 75 to 96 prescriptions, but it is difficult to work out the reasons for this jump. It might reflect a real rise in the number of opiate users, or it might be evidence of a greater degree of contact between the Northern Road Centre and the drug users. Changes in the numbers of notified addicts usually lag behind changes on the street, by several years: it takes some time for a user to come to the attention of the medical services. So if the increase in prescriptions is an indicator of increasing numbers of users, it is likely to be indicating a change that took place some time ago, and not something that happened in the last 12 months. On the other hand, if the reason for the big increase is that a greater proportion of addicts went to the Northern Road Centre, then the change is one that really had happened in the year. The impression we have from our own contact with the local drug scene is that users were more willing to go to the Northern Road Centre than they had been in the past, and evidence from probation officers and social workers does not suggest that there had been any overall increase in the number of local users.

General practitioners in the Wessex health region

In mid-1985 a national survey of general practitioners was carried out by Alan Glanz and Colin Taylor of the Institute of Psychiatry with the aim of gauging the extent of their contact with opiate users. They contacted 1,166 doctors (five per cent of all GPs) and received 845 replies, a response of 72 per cent. In the Wessex Health Region, which is spread across the counties of Hampshire, Dorset, Wiltshire and Avon, 48 out of 54 doctors replied, a response of 89 per cent.

The GPs were asked how many opiate users they had seen in the previous four weeks. In the Wessex region 5 of the 48 doctors had seen a user in that period. From this, Glanz and Taylor calculated that the total number of opiate users visiting GPs over one year was 72.8 per 100,000 of the population aged 16 to 44 in the region. By comparison, the survey showed the national figure to be 204.3 per 100,000.

There are two points to be made about these results. First, the Wessex figure is much lower than the national figure. This adds weight to the conclusion we have drawn from the official statistics that the counties in Wessex, including Hampshire, have a lower level of opiate addiction than the national one. Secondly, the numbers of drug users estimated by Glanz and Taylor to be in contact with GPs was much higher than the numbers shown in the Home Office figures. Glanz and Taylor say that the difference can be explained by the different case definitions used (they asked about people seen with 'problems associated with misuse of heroin or other opiate drugs', a wider definition than the one used for the official statistics), by under-notification of addicts to the Home Office by GPs, and by double-counting of users in the survey.

Glanz and Taylor point out that the main aim of their survey was to look at how often GPs had contact with drug abusers. Their general conclusion is important: whatever the reason for the discrepancy between the survey figures and the Home Office figures, the latter source is an inadequate indicator of the real demand for general practitioner services by opiate misusers, which is considerable.

Prosecutions and seizures of drugs by the police

Possession or supply of most 'street drugs' is illegal, and a large proportion of users at some time have dealings with the police. Statistics of proceedings against drug abusers and seizures of illegal drugs provide indicators of the level of drug use in an area, but only in the broadest terms. The statistics are influenced not only by the number of users and frequency of use, but also by the strategies and priorities of the police, by their effectiveness and by their luck.

Prosecutions

Table 2.5 shows the numbers of cautions and prosecutions for Hampshire and for the Police Division that most closely corresponds to the Portsmouth and Havant local authority areas. Before 1984 this was the South Eastern Division, a slightly larger area than the Eastern Division, which has existed since 1984 and is almost exactly the area covered by this study.

Table 2.5 Prosecutions and cautions under 1971 Misuse of Drugs Act, 1979-1986

	79	80	81	82	83	84	85	86
All offences								
Hampshire	572	575	688	636	734	640	806	807
per cent that were cautions	3	2	7	2	4	7	11	14
Eastern Division						323	143	187
S.Eastern Division	228	177	190	253	313			
per cent that were cautions	1	1	1	1	2	9	7	16
Supply offences								
Hampshire	*no statistics prior to 84*					144	161	215
Eastern Division						90	45	76
Prisons in Hampshire: Inmates dealt with under Prison Rules for Drug Offences	*no statistics prior to 83*				127	95	123	119

(Note: these are not included in any of the above figures.)

In the county, there were 572 cautions and prosecutions in 1979, rising to 807 in 1986. This general upward trend was not steady: the total fell in 1982 and 1984, and the 1986 figure was the same as in the previous year. The local figures show no overall trend, falling then rising between 1979 and 1983, then falling again: the annual numbers range between 143 and 323. Over the whole eight-year period about a third of the proceedings were in the Portsmouth and Havant area.

One distinct trend is the growth in the number of cautions as a proportion of all proceedings. This rose both in the county and locally. This is in line with a national trend in favour of cautioning people found in possession of small amounts of cannabis.

The table also shows the number of supply offences within the total number of offences since 1984. In the Portsmouth and Havant areas a rather higher proportion of proceedings were for supply offences than in the rest of the county - 32 per cent of proceedings as opposed to 23 per cent. This could indicate a greater extent of drug supply business based in the area, or reflect a different approach by the officers working in the area. However, it should be remembered that these figures are only available for three years, and should therefore be regarded with some care.

Public attention is often drawn to the availablity of illicit drugs within prisons. The table shows the number of prison inmates in Hampshire dealt with under the rules for drug offences from 1983 to 1986. There is no discernable trend over the four years, but there was a substantial number of offences, averaging 116 each year.

Seizures

Table 2.6 shows the annual numbers of police seizures of various drugs. The figures are given separately for the UK, for Hampshire and for the Eastern/South Eastern Police Division. The national statistics are from the Home Office, while the local figures are from the Hampshire Constabulary, and so there are different gaps in the series. All the numbers refer to actual seizures, and not to amounts seized or numbers of people involved.

Table 2.6 Police seizures of drugs, 1980-1986

	80	81	82	83	84	85	86
United Kingdom (source: *Home Office Statistics*)							
Heroin	612	731	848	1745	2800	3002	na
Diconal	259	368	428	292	162	92	na
Cocaine	365	396	314	558	739	509	na
Amphetamine	645	1036	1605	2283	2715	3245	na
LSD	243	356	430	474	574	448	na
Cannabis (herbal)	7201	6765	7077	6591	7658	8166	na
Cannabis (resin)	6216	8131	9985	13231	13089	13732	na
Total seizures	14946	16667	19014	22745	25233	26674	na
Hampshire (source: *Hampshire Constabulary*)							
Heroin/Opiates	17	14	17	24	48	37	37
Diconal	30	31	20	17	4	9	6
Cocaine	na	na	5	8	7	2	5
Amphetamine	18	35	66	87	88	139	101
LSD	5	6	20	13	14	10	12
Cannabis	447	514	406	487	488	520	532
Eastern/South Eastern Division (source: *Hampshire Constabulary*)							
Heroin/Opiates	na	6	4	13	28	9	24
Diconal	na	7	3	5	3	-	5
Cocaine	na	na	1	5	1	-	3
Amphetamine	na	11	22	40	43	31	22
LSD	na	1	6	2	3	1	4
Cannabis	na	150	165	204	233	94	112

The national figures show big increases between 1980 and 1985 in the numbers of heroin seizures (612 to 3002) and amphetamine seizures (645 to 3245). Although the increases are less regular, there were also increases in the seizures of cocaine (365 to 509, with a peak of 739 in 1984), LSD (243 to 448, with a 1984 peak of 574) and cannabis (7,201 to 8,166 for herbal cannabis, and 6,216 to 13,732 for resin). The total number of controlled drugs seizures by the police rose fairly steadily over the five-year period, from 14,946 to 26,674. Against this trend is the decrease in the number of seizures of dipipanone (Diconal) from 259 in 1980 to 92 in 1985. This follows the change of prescribing policy away from Diconal tablets.

In Hampshire there was a slow and uneven increase in cannabis seizures (from 447 in 1980 to 532 in 1986), and a substantial rise in amphetamine seizures (from 18 to 101). Heroin and other opiate seizures also rose unevenly from 17 to 37, while Diconal seizures fell from 30 to 6. These trends are all broadly in line with the national picture, although in Hampshire the increases were slower for cannabis and heroin than they were nationally. In Hampshire cocaine seizures and LSD seizures were relatively few, and seemed to follow no trend; in 1986 there were 5 seizures of cocaine and 12 seizures of LSD.

Looking at the Portsmouth and Havant area, it is difficult to discern any clear trends, except an uneven increase in heroin and other opiate seizures. Cannabis seizures seem to have peaked, at over 200, in 1983 and 1984, and were down to 112 in 1986. There were 22 amphetamine seizures in 1986 (again after peaking in 1983 and 1984, at over 40), 5 seizures of Diconal, 4 seizures of LSD and 3 of cocaine. There were 29 seizures of other drugs.

Agency caseloads

One of the main tasks of the project was to collate information on drug users known to the Northern Road Centre, the probation service, and the social services, and to see what could be learned about the degree to which these agencies have a common client base.

Each of these three agencies has contact with some of the drug users in the area. One agency does not necessarily see the same users as another, but there is some overlap. We can therefore look at the cases known to the agencies as three different but interlocking groups of local drug users.

Drug users come to the notice of the three agencies for different reasons. Northern Road is of course different from the other two because it deals only with drug users. To become a client of Northern Road, a user has to be referred by another agency or by a doctor, or has to seek its help voluntarily. To become a client of the probation service, a user has to be convicted of a crime, but not necessarily a drugs offence. Users become clients of the social services for any of a wide range of reasons, but it is unlikely that drug use will be the primary factor. The work of the social services departments is determined both by statutory responsibilities and by local priorities, and drug users can come to the notice of social workers as members of families in difficulty, as mentally ill persons, as adolescents in care or under supervision, or even as elderly persons.

Collection of data

PSI obtained information from Northern Road on all its clients. From the probation offices and social services offices we obtained information on those clients who were drug users. The first period selected was July 1986. Probation officers and social workers were issued with short forms to fill in for each drug user among their clients; null-return forms were filled in by those who did not know of any users. Probation officers and social workers were asked to give users' names and dates of birth, but many were reluctant to do this for reasons of confidentiality. They were therefore given the option to supply initials rather than names. The definition of 'drugs' was broad: it included solvents and prescribed tranquillisers where there was intoxication that impaired behaviour; alcohol, however, was not counted as a drug if used on its own. The forms were collected by PSI and kept under lock and key, and were seen only by members of the research team. After the project they will be destroyed. The forms were analysed first by looking at the total numbers of users known to each agency, then by looking at the overlaps between them.

Northern Road Centre

There were 191 cases on the Centre's register: we categorised their drug of principal use as follows:

Opiates	129
Cannabis only	2
Other drugs	45
Not recorded	15
TOTAL	191

The 'other drugs' category includes 18 people using prescribed drugs - usually tranquillisers. The rest were mostly amphetamine users, but there was also a small number of people using solvents, amylnitrite, and cough linctus.

Probation service

The total number of users reported was 80. We obtained information on all the drugs that probation officers thought their clients were taking, rather than the principal drug alone. Most were taking more than one drug, and although a relatively small proportion were taking cannabis alone, a majority were cannabis users. Our classification is therefore by the most serious drug mentioned; any opiate or opioid use puts clients in the opiate category, regardless of whatever else is taken, and the 'cannabis only' category excludes all other drugs entirely. Clients were categorised as follows:

Opiates	36
Cannabis only	15
Other drugs	28
Not recorded	1
TOTAL	80

Two-thirds of the 'other' group were amphetamine users. It also included a small group of clients using solvents (4) and a small group abusing tranquillisers (3).

Social services

The total number of users reported was 34. They were categorised as follows, again by most serious drug:

Opiates	9
Cannabis only	5
Other drugs	19
Not recorded	1
TOTAL	34

About half of the clients used cannabis, with or without other drugs. The 'other drugs' category was more of a mixture than in the case of the probation clients. Just under half were amphetamine users, and several of the amphetamine users also took other drugs such as barbiturates and LSD. Five clients abused tranquillisers or painkillers. Five clients were solvent abusers.

Overlaps

Table 2.7 shows the overlap between the Northern Road Centre and the probation service. It can seen that of the 36 opiate users known to probation officers, 22 were on the Northern Road register (61 per cent); of the 15 clients who used only cannabis, none were on the Northern Road register; of the 29 other users, 7 were on the Northern Road register (24 per cent). Opiate users were therefore more likely than other drug users to be known to both agencies. Looking at the figures the other way around, we see that 15 per cent of all Northern Road clients were known to the probation service.

Table 2.7 Overlap between Probation and Northern Road clients

	Known to Probation only	Known to Probation and Northern Road	Known to Northern Road only
Opiates	14	22	107
Cannabis	15	0	2
Other	21	7	38
Unspecified	1	0	15
TOTAL	51	29	162

Between the social services and the Northern Road Centre. It can be seen that of the 9 opiate users known to social workers, 6 were registered with Northern Road; their 5 cannabis users were not known to Northern Road; and 3 of their 20 other drug users were known to Northern Road. This pattern is rather similar to the one shown above: opiate users were much more likely than other users to be known to both agencies. Overall, however, only 5 per cent of Northern Road were clients of the social services.

Table 2.8 Overlap between Social Services and Northern Road clients

	Known to Social Services only	Known to Social Services and Northern Road	Known to Northern Road only
Opiates	3	6	122
Cannabis	5	0	2
Other	16	3	41
Unspecified	1	0	17
TOTAL	25	9	182

Table 2.9 compares the drug user clients of the Social Services and the Probation Service. The overlap is small, and exists only for opiate users.

Table 2.9 Overlap between Social Services and Probation clients

	Known to Social Services only	Known to Social Services and Probation	Known to Probation only
Opiates	7	2	34
Cannabis	5	0	15
Other	19	0	28
Unspecified	1	0	1
TOTAL	32	2	78

Overall these figures demonstrate that the Northern Road Clinic saw a fairly high proportion of the opiate users known to the two other agencies - 26 out of 43 found in our caseload reviews (60 per cent).

It is noticable that the overlap between the agencies for drugs other than opiates and opioids is much smaller. Of 47 'other' users known to the probation service and the social services, only 10 were known to Northern Road (21 per cent), and there was no overlap at all in the case of those who use only cannabis. This suggests that Northrn Road sees a much smaller proportion of the total illicit drug user population than it does of the opiate users. This is not surprising: although the clinic is open to users of all drugs, its priorities are with the more serious drugs, and most of its clients are users of heroin, methadone or Diconal. In the general population, most illicit drug users are not taking these drugs.

Police data

At an early stage of the project we intended to ask the police to conduct a type of caseload review: to fill in forms for every drug-related incident that came to officers' attention over a given period. Although the police were willing to go ahead with this plan, we decided that it would deliver no better information than the police's own drug information forms, to which we were given access.

The DDA.5A form, headed 'Drug Incident Report', is meant to be filled in whenever any police officer (not just those in the drugs squad) comes across any incident or information related to drug misuse. The officer records details of the incident, including the name and age of the the person or persons involved. PSI was given confidential access to the forms for the months of April and July 1986, for the Portsmouth and Havant area. Both sets of forms were analysed for the types of incidents recorded. The July forms were also analysed by the initials and date of birth of the individuals involved, for comparison with the agency caseload reviews. All of this information will be destroyed at the end of the project, and no-one outside the research team has seen it.

Incidents and drugs

The incidents described on the forms were each classified by PSI as one of the following: a stop, when an officer has stopped and searched a suspected drug user in the street (although not necessarily found any drugs); a drugs arrest or search of premises, when officers have gone out with the intention of arresting a person for a drugs offence or searching their home; a call to a scene or arrest for non-drug offence, when officers have been called to an incident or apprehended someone for purposes unrelated to drugs, then find that there is a drugs connection (usually by finding drugs on the offender); or, finally, information received, which includes telephone calls to the drug squad and information given to other officers in the course of their work.

Analysis of the forms was not entirely straightforward. The information is collected for operational purposes, rather than as a research project. A few of the incidents were only tenuously related to drugs; some of the information given by the public is shown by later investigation to be malicious, intended to cause trouble for an innocent individual; some of the 'information received' comes in quantities too large to fit on a single form, and therefore it is sometimes hard to tell where one form ends and another begins; and some of the information relates to people and events outside the area. The PSI researcher went through the forms with a senior officer of the drugs squad who answered queries and helped decode the information; during this process a number of forms were excluded from the analysis because they were not directly to do with drugs, because the information was bogus, or because they did not fall within the geographical area of the study. It should be noted that one incident form can contain the details of more than one person: for example, some of the arrests, counted here as single incidents, involve two or more people.

The majority of the forms related to information received, rather than specific incidents involving drugs or drug users. Fifty-four per cent of April's 68 forms, and 71 per cent of July's 97 forms concerned information received. In addition there were several batches of information from drugs squad officers. The number of information-only forms was higher in July than in April, but the remaining forms show a remarkably similar pattern of stops, arrests, and calls to scenes. In April there were 19 stops, 3 drugs arrest incidents, and 9 calls to scenes, and in July these numbers were almost the same.

	April	July
Stops	19	15
Drugs arrests or searches of premises	3	5
Calls to scene or arrests for non-drug offences	9	8
Information	37	69
TOTAL	68	97

It is worth looking in more detail at the nature of the incidents and at the drugs involved. For this analysis we have added together the two months' cases. Among the 34 stop incidents there were 9 arrests for drug offences, one person found in possession of prescribed drugs, and 24 negative searches. Among these negative searches, 8 revealed evidence that we can take as indication of involvement with drugs. These items were sets of small plastic bags, clean syringes, numerous bundles of money in small amounts, packets of cigarette papers with pieces torn off to make 'roaches' (rolled cardboard filters), long cigarette papers with cannabis motifs, a bottomless milk bottle along with a small stove (equipment used to burn cannabis for direct inhalation), and empty paper packets like those in which drugs are sold. In one case the user admitted swallowing the evidence.

The 9 stop arrests were for possession of heroin (1), cannabis (5), and cannabis with amphetamine or pemoline (2); the type of drug could not be determined from one of the forms. The 8 drugs arrests/searches break down as follows: 2 arrests for possession of cannabis, one for possession of amphetamine, one for a forged prescription, one arrest of 2 people for possession of cannabis and capsules (unidentified), one arrest of 2 people for the possession of heroin, and 2 searches of premises. During one of them, Pemoline tablets, plastic bags and cash were found, and someone was later found in possession of cannabis and amphetamine; the other search was negative.

The 17 calls to scenes were a mixed bag. In 11 of them, people arrested for non-drugs offences were found with evidence of drug-taking: cannabis was found on 8 of them, and one also had burnt silver paper; two had methadone, one with cannabis as well; in 2 cases offenders admitted drug use; one case was an overdose collapse; and 3 other cases involved people already known to the police as users.

It is clear from these breakdowns that a relatively large proportion of the drug incidents recorded by the police involve cannabis. Of the stops, arrests and calls to scenes, 25 involve cannabis, and 19 of them involve cannabis alone; this is out of a total of 38 incidents where the drugs were identified on the forms.

A majority of the forms that contained only information (rather than a record of an incident) were about dealers and user-dealers. About 30 per cent were about cannabis, 30 per cent were about opiates, about 10 per cent were about other drugs and about 30 per cent did not specify the drugs concerned.

Overlap analysis

From the July 1986 DDA.5A forms we recorded where possible the initials and date of birth of the individuals concerned, and we have made some comparisons with the lists of users obtained from the probation officers, social workers, and the Northern Road Centre.

The procedure assumes that all the people in the police records were themselves users. We know that many of them were dealers, and therefore this assumption may not be true in all cases; however, we also know that most dealers are drug users, and the analysis is therefore unlikely to be severely damaged by the inclusion of a small number of non-user dealers.

There are serious problems, however, with the extent to which we can make confident identifications of users on other lists. The DDA forms do not always give very full details of dates of birth (often these were simply not available to the officer at the time), and the drugs involved in an incident may not be the same drugs listed by another agency. For example, consider a fictitious person TS, born 5.4.53, identified as an opiate user by the Northern Road Centre. Like most heroin users, he also smokes cannabis. A police officer stops and searches him, but he quickly swallows the small amount of cannabis he has with him; the officer does not arrest him. Later the officer makes out a DDA.5A form and estimates the user's age as 37; he was actually only 34 at the time, but the mistake is understandable because of the ageing effect of drugs and alcohol. The two sets of identifying information are:

Northern Road	Police
TS 5.4.53 Opiates	TS Age 37 Cannabis

A sensible approach would be to regard this near miss as a possible overlap. We have therefore produced two versions of the overlap, one based on certain identifications and the other based on certain plus possible identifications. A further problem is the number of DDA forms that do not specify the drug involved - about 30 per cent. This not only makes identification more hazardous, but produces a wide range of error for the estimates derived from the overlap. We therefore give both ends of the range for each of the estimates.

Table 2.10 Opiates: police-agency overlap

	Agency only	Agency and Police	Police only
Definite identifications			
Northern Road	119	10	19
Probation	32	4	25
Social Services	9	0	29
Definite plus possible identifications			
Northern Road	107	22	18
Probation	28	8	23
Social Services	6	3	29

Table 2.10 shows the definite and possible overlaps for opiate users. If we look first at the definite cases, Northern Road and probation appear to have some opiate users in common with the police DDA records, although the social services have none. However, if the possible cases are included, the overlap is substantial - for example, over half of the opiate users noted on the DDA forms are known to Northern Road.

Table 2.11 shows the overlap for other drugs identified, excluding cannabis. There is only one positively identified user common to the police and the social services, and none common to the police and the other agencies. Taking into account the possible identifications, however, there is some overlap both for Northern Road and for probation. This result is in line with the comparisons of the agencies' caseloads: although some opiate users are known to more than one, the same is true for very few users of other drugs.

Table 2.11 Other drugs (excluding Cannabis): police-agency overlap

	Agency only	Agency and Police	Police only
Definite identifications			
Northern Road	45	0	15
Probation	28	0	15
Social Services	18	1	14
Definite plus possible identifications			
Northern Road	43	2	13
Probation	24	4	11
Social Services	18	1	14

Estimating totals from the overlaps

In total, our caseload review for July 1986 reveals between 161 and 201 unique individual opiate users who featured in the records of the Northern Road Centre, the probation service, the social services and the police. There are obviously many more users who do not come into contact with these organisations, or who did not appear on their records during that month, but we can use the overlap data to make an estimate of the total size of the user population. One technique for estimating the numbers of drug users in a locality is known as the 'indicator dilution method' and also as the 'capture-recapture method'. It relies on a statistical procedure developed for estimating the numbers of fish in lakes.

For fish, the method is this. A batch of fish is caught, tagged and returned to the water; another batch is later caught from the same lake and the number of tagged fish in the second batch is counted. It can be shown by simple mathematics that the total number of fish in the lake is equal to the size of the two batches multiplied together, then divided by the number of tagged fish found in the second batch. This is simple and elegant, but it works only if the two samples are random and independent of each other, and if they are big enough to produce a substantial number of tagged fish in the second batch. For drug users, the corresponding method is to obtain two lists of names from different sources and to see how many people are on both lists. The method was used by the North London Drug Indicators Project, comparing the numbers of addict deaths, hospital admissions, and users whose names appeared in the local press. For 1982, their estimates were in the range of 2,148 to 2,435 opiate users in Camden and Islington.

If the Northern Road, probation and social services clients are regarded as independent samples of drug users, the overlaps would suggest that Northern Road sees over half of all the area's opiate users. Unfortunately they cannot be said to be truly independent samples, for it is likely that a number of the users went to Northern Road as a result of encouragement or referral by the other agencies. Consequently, these indicator-dilution calculations are bound to give an underestimate of the total number of users in the area.

Between a third and a half of known opiate users in the police records were Northern Road clients; however, if we assume all the people for whom no drug is identified are opiate users, the proportion known to Northern Road falls to between just under a fifth and a third. It is unlikely that these unidentified drugs are in every case heroin, so this proportion is unlikely to be quite as low as a fifth. The samples of users known to the police and Northern Road are much more likely to be independent of each other than in the case of the other comparisons.

Table 2.12 summarises the calculations based on the overlaps between the different organisations. On each line the smaller number is based on only the positively identified opiate users, while the larger number assumes all 'not known' drugs are opiates. Clearly some of the estimates, such as the lower ends of the ranges (b), (g) and (h), are of little use: they are lower than the total number of actual users we have identified. They are based on large overlaps which are the result of users appearing in one of the samples by virtue of being in another. As mentioned above, a general problem of estimates based on the indicator-dilution method is their vulnerability to non-independence of samples.

If we look at the higher estimates, we see that the highest are those involving the overlaps between the police records, Northern Road and the probation service. The range of these estimates is large, from about 240 to 778. The true figure is unlikely to be at the low end of this range, since this estimate is not a lot larger than the total number of individual users identified in the caseload reviews, but it is also unlikely to be at the top of the range, since that estimate is based on the assumption that all the users of unrecorded drugs are heroin users. Whatever assumptions are used, it is clear than the lists of users that are most independent of each other are those from Northern Road and from the police. The estimates of the total user population calculated from their overlap are in the range 235 to 778, and the best estimate is likely to be somewhere below the middle of this range, between 450 and 550.

One area in which this analysis is deficient is in its coverage of users aged under 20. Very few of the opiate users identified were under 20, although the schools survey suggests that there are some teenage heroin users, and our own interviews with users seem to confirm this. Older users were more likely than younger users to be known to the Northern Road Centre, the probation service and the police; the social services knew about some younger drug users, but most of them were not using opiates.

Table 2.12 Summary of caseload reviews, July 1986 - Opiates

Individual opiate users identified:		
NRC	129 - 144	
Probation	36 - 37	
Social Services	9 - 10	
Police	29 - 55	
Total unique individual users (excluding all definite overlaps)	165 - 201	
Total unique individual users (excluding all definite and possible overlaps)	161 - 198	
Indicator dilution estimates of total opiate user population ...		
... based on all definite overlaps:		
(a) Northern Road - Probation Overlap		211 - 242
(b) Northern Road - Social Services Overlap		194 - 240
(c) Social Services - Probation Overlap		162 - 185
(d) Northern Road - Police Overlap		374 - 778
(e) Probation - Police Overlap		261 - 500
... based on all definite and possible overlaps:		
(f) Northern Road - Police Overlap		235 - 393
(g) Probation - Police Overlap		140 - 236
(h) Social Services - Police Overlap		96 - 180

Changes 1986 - 1987

We have already seen that the number of people in Portsmouth and Havant who collected opiate prescriptions from chemists rose between 1986 and 1987. There were 75 people recorded in 1986 and 93 in 1987 (this figure differs slightly from that given in Table 2.4 because of the omission of two prescriptions for other controlled drugs). Is this sharp rise the result of a wave of new addictions or of a greater proportion of previous addicts coming under medical supervision? Several pieces of information suggest that it is the latter.

Analysis of the prescriptions data shows that most of the new prescriptions are the result of contact with Northern Road. In fact the net increase of nearly 20 prescriptions is the result of much larger gross changes - about 20 people disappeared from the list between 1986 and 1987 and about 40 new people appeared, nearly all of whom had been to Northern Road. Recent changes in the treatment policy at Northern Road had made the place much more accessible to users, and the number of clients increased dramatically as a result. It appears that these policy changes lie behind the increase in the number of prescriptions.

As far as we can tell from the prescriptions list, none of the new people were aged under 21, and most were over 25. There is therefore no evidence that the newly-notified users were the product of any growth in teenage heroin use. Although some of the dates of birth were missing from the data (about a third), a majority of those we had were over 30, and this suggests that the 'new users' were in fact old hands who were approaching the drug services.

In July 1987 we repeated the caseload reviews for the probation and social services, this time not asking for names or initials: in other words, the review was a simple head-count of users known to the services, one year after the first review described above. The procedures were simpler than in 1986 and as a result the social workers and probation officers responded more quickly. We were surprised to find that the total number of drug users in their count was lower than in 1986 by about a third. Between the two services a total of 29 opiate users were identified in 1987, compared with an equivalent count of 45 in 1986. Thirty-two users of other drugs (excluding cannabis alone) were identified in 1987, compared with 47 the year before. The total for cannabis alone also fell from 20 to 13. We are confident that this fall in the number of known users was not the result of poorer data-recording by individual probation officers and social workers, nor a product of any changes in the recording procedures: if anything we would have expected the figures to have risen as a result of the changes. These results indicate, therefore, that the number of probation and social services clients using illicit drugs fell during the period that the number of Northern Road clients rose. This is further indication that the rise in the number of notified users is not an indicator of a burgeoning drugs epidemic, but instead shows that more of the old users were seeking help.

The prevalence of illicit drug use - a final caution

The elusive facts

Investigating the scale and nature of illicit drug taking is a frustrating enterprise. The people directly involved, whether they are buying drugs or selling them, have every reason to keep their activities secret. It is not possible to stand back and view the drugs scene as a whole, and we therefore have to rely on disparate pieces of information that we try to fit together, like a particularly troublesome jig-saw puzzle. When an ordinary jig-saw is being assembled, there is a picture to work towards; the box contains all of the pieces; the size of the picture is known in advance; and we can be sure that all of the pieces will eventually fit together. None of this is true for the investigation of illicit drugs. We are trying to work out the picture from the pieces as we go along; many of the pieces are missing, and we have no advance idea how many there ought to be; and we find that some of the pieces simply do not fit together.

The only facts we can be sure about are the officially-recorded events when drug users come into contact with the legal world and the medical world, but the meaning of those facts for determining the contours of the larger world of drug abuse is in each case open to question: the statistics of notifications, arrests and seizures all give useful information, but they all mean different things in different areas and at different times, depending on the policies and practices of the services for drug users and of the police. The impressions of the people who work with drug users are also useful, but they do not always agree with each other, and their views are limited by the perspectives of their working relationships with users. Above all, the drugs workers, the caring agencies and the police tend to see people who are in trouble. Those who steer clear of the law, and whose lives remain on an even keel, avoid official attention.

Getting close to the users themselves is only part of the answer. The view from the street is not necessarily any clearer than the view from anywhere else: we found that users' estimates of the numbers involved in the local drugs scene were as varied as any others. The information we obtained from speaking to users is invaluable, but not in direct quantitative terms. They provided information on the development of their own drug use, on the lives they lead, and on the way things work in the local drugs world, or, rather, in the part of it they inhabit. Users see their own friends and business contacts, and generalise in the same way as anyone else, with assumptions that are sometimes shaky. Surprisingly, the estimates made by people who have been involved in selling drugs can be as suspect as others: during this study one of the wildest estimates of the local population of heroin users, so large as to be wrong by a wide margin, was made by an ex-dealer. The fact that users' views on numbers cannot be relied upon any more than anyone else's is perhaps an important finding.

Not just heroin

People are concerned about heroin. They see advertising posters showing syringes encrusted with dried blood as well as images of teenage addicts with a deathly pallor and spotty skin. Television programmes have shown heart-breaking documentary footage of young lives wrecked by heroin dependence, followed up with 'phone-ins' for worried parents and teenagers.

As a result of this publicity, the word 'drugs' for many people now means heroin. And yet heroin is still a very small part of the illicit drugs scene: cannabis seizures are almost ten times as common as heroin seizures, and four-fifths of legal proceedings under the drugs legislation concern cannabis. The number of heroin users is small compared with the number who use only cannabis. In the next section of the report we shall see that even among school pupils in Portsmouth and Havant there are hundreds of cannabis users, while heroin users can be numbered only in tens. To understand the drugs world it is vital to grasp this point: the drugs scene is not one single group of people who take every drug that is going. There are different groups of different sizes taking different drugs, and if they are linked together it is by virtue of the fact that they are all involved in illegal activity. Although this report concentrates on heroin and other opiates, they are used by only a small proportion of those who take illicit drugs.

What are we counting?

Some of this section of the report has been concerned with an attempt to determine the numbers of visible drug users in Portsmouth and Havant during a single month. If it concerned a whole year, the number would be bigger. This illustrates a general point about estimating the level of drug abuse: at a single point in time there will be fewer drug users than the total counted over a period of time. As time passes, some people stop using while other people start. It is therefore too simple to ask 'how many heroin users are there in Portsmouth and Havant'; the question has to include a time period. We have been careful in this section of the report to indicate the period of time that each of the statistics refers to.

The term 'addict' causes further difficulties for counting the number of users. There is a widely-held notion that all heroin users are driven by a physical craving to take it on a daily basis, but this is true only for a proportion of users. Others take heroin at regular but infrequent intervals, demonstrating that it is not the discomfort of withdrawal that leads them to continue with the drug: for example, some people use heroin only at weekends, and they do not match up to the popular image of junkies. While a substantial proportion of opiate users do have a daily habit and a physical dependence, there is a periphery of less serious users, some on the verge of dependence but others taking the drug only casually. This mixture of people with very different levels of habit means that the figures we have arrived at in this report have to be used carefully.

Service provision and the visibility of the drugs problem

There is a danger in using the numbers of medically notified users to measure the extent of a local drugs problem. The existence of local services for drug users tends to raise the numbers who are using prescribed drugs, and therefore any area with well developed services will appear to have a worse 'problem' if notifications are used as an indicator of the general size of the opiate user population. In addition, any facility for people with problems tends to make them more visible as a group. In this respect the people providing the drug services cannot win: the more they do, the more the statistics escalate. In an area where the problem is ignored, the statistics hardly exist, and people can continue to ignore it. The recent growth in the number of opiate prescriptions in the Portsmouth and Havant area is a case in point. It is likely that what appears to be an escalation of the drugs problem is exactly the opposite: the number of users could have remained more or less the same, while a larger proportion have come forward to seek treatment.

At first sight it might seem that there is a substantial local drugs problem when compared with the rest of Hampshire: within the county about half of the users of prescribed opiates live in Portsmouth and Havant. But the services for drug users have a long history in the Portsmouth area, and are the best developed in the county. The local concentration of legally-supplied users is therefore inevitable. How this fact relates to the numbers of illegally-supplied users living in different parts of Hampshire is problematical. Analysis of the annual figures for seizures and proceedings shows that the legal events associated with illicit drug use are not so heavily concentrated in the Portsmouth and Havant area, adding weight to the argument that illegal drug use is spread more evenly throughout the county than is legal opiate use.

3 THE SURVEY OF YOUNG PEOPLE

During the autumn and winter of 1986-1987, PSI carried out a survey of young people in schools and colleges in Portsmouth and Havant. The study, organised in conjuction with the Portsmouth and South East Hampshire Health Education Unit, was designed to provide information on young people's leisure activities, life-styles and views, and to gauge their use of alcohol, tobacco and illicit drugs.

Origins, aims and methods

Early in our general study of local drug use it became clear that the agencies dealing with drug users were unable to supply details of many who were under the age of 20. The Northern Road Advice Centre, the probation service, the social services and the police did not have contact with many drug users who were new and inexperienced, or those who used infrequently. PSI therefore decided to mount a survey of young people in schools, in order to get an idea of the extent of drug use among local teenagers. Around the same time, the Health Education Unit was planning a schools survey to provide information to help plan its work among young people and, as the Unit was particularly concerned with alcohol, tobacco and drug use, the obvious step was to combine forces in a joint survey.

The survey sample

Twenty-three schools and colleges in the Portsmouth and Havant local authority areas were included in the survey. These were middle schools, secondary schools, and colleges for students aged 16 and over, all falling under the aegis of the Portsmouth and South East Hampshire Areas of the Hampshire Education Authority. The schools were selected at random. From each middle school in the sample a single class was selected; from each year group in the secondary schools one class was chosen; from each of the colleges and sixth forms, students were chosen at random to make up the equivalent of two classes. The classes were largely picked at random, although efforts were made to ensure that a representative range of abilities was represented in the sample. Once a class was chosen for the sample, all of its members were included in the survey.

With the help of the Portsmouth and South East Hampshire Area Education Officers, PSI requested the co-operation of the schools' head teachers, and 23 of the 25 selected agreed to participate. Once the classes were selected, parents of the school pupils were sent letters explaining that the survey was to take place and giving them the chance to withdraw their child. In the event, few pupils were withdrawn. Older pupils and students were themselves informed in advance of the survey by letter. The final number of pupils and students in the survey was 1,065. Two questionnaires were left out of the analysis because they were obviously filled in mischievously, and the analysis is therefore based on a sample of 1,063 pupils.

The questionnaires

The information was collected using simple self-completion questionnaire forms. Four different versions of the form were produced, taking into account the reading and comprehension abilities of the different age groups and expected differences in leisure activities, although the same basic information was sought in each of them.

Pupils were asked about their age and sex, the district in which they lived, and their parents' employment. There were also questions about: pupils' leisure activities over the last week, their reading habits and their favourite TV programmes; their pocket money and money they earned; how much they agreed and disagreed with their parents about a number of subjects; their chances of passing their exams, and getting a job; the likelihood of their taking risks, such as playing truant, getting in a fight, or accepting a lift from a stranger; their use of alcohol, tobacco and illicit drugs; and the drug use of people they knew.

A small pilot survey was conducted in advance of the main study. This was to test how well the questionnaire worked. Few changes were made as a result of the pilot; in fact the changes were so small that we were able to include the data from the pilot in the main survey data; this helped to make up for the numbers lost from the two schools that did not participate.

Each questionnaire was seven or eight pages long, and took most pupils about 15 minutes to fill in. An example of the questionnaire is shown in an appendix to this report.

Conduct of the survey

The questionnaires were completed in classrooms or school halls. Every attempt was made to help pupils feel confident that they could give truthful answers without fear of any repercussions; above all, we wanted those who had taken illicit drugs to feel happy about admitting this on the questionnaire form. We were also concerned to stop pupils using the survey as an opportunity to show off in front of their classmates by pretending they had taken drugs. Questionnaires were given out and completed under the supervision of a PSI researcher and with the teacher present; the researcher's tasks were to explain the purpose of the survey and to deter pupils from conferring and seeing each other's forms. The forms did not ask for the pupils' names and, once completed, they were sealed in blank envelopes by the pupils. The teachers were not permitted to see the forms - in case they recognised the pupil's handwriting - and pupils were informed of this before they filled them in. Pupils were told that the survey was anonymous and confidential, and were given an introduction explaining the purposes of the survey. Once sealed in envelopes, the forms were returned at once to PSI for computer analysis.

The anonymity of the survey was essential, but it did cause a problem: where pupils filled in a question wrongly, or left one out altogether, we were unable to go back to them for clarification. Usually, in a survey where informants are identifiable, researchers return to fill these gaps in the data. Fortunately, most of the questions in this survey were filled in correctly by most of the pupils and students; but there are some gaps. In particular, we had difficulty classifying some of the parents' occupations from our informants' brief (and sometimes strange) descriptions.

Basic characteristics of the pupils

Age and sex

Table 3.1 shows the age and sex breakdown of the 1,063 informants. Their ages ranged from 11 to 19; there was a fairly even number in each age group up to and including the 16 year-olds, but after that the numbers tailed off, and there were only 43 aged over 17. In the main analysis of the survey findings we have divided the informants into four age groups: 11-year-olds (14%), 12 and 13-year-olds (33%), 14 and 15-year-olds (32%), and 16 to 19-year-olds (21%).

Table 3.1 Survey of young people: sex and age

	Number	%
Male	483	45
Female	579	55
Age		
11	141	13
12	199	19
13	152	14
14	164	15
15	180	17
16	107	10
17	77	7
18	40	4
19	3	*
TOTAL	1,063	100

The sample is about half boys and half girls, with the girls in a small majority. Some of the imbalance results from the selection of classes for inclusion in the survey: in some of the year groups we unintentionally chose a greater number of classes and tutor groups that comprised more girls than boys (this was definitely the case for the 16 to 19-year-olds). Some of the imbalance, however, cannot be explained in this way and may well be the result of a greater rate of absence and truancy among boys. Other surveys of school pupils (to which we refer later) have suffered from the same problem - girls were in the majority by several percentage points. The loss of a few boys would not be a problem as long as they were not different from the boys included in the survey, but we cannot be sure of this. There is evidence from the survey itself that truants might be more likely to be involved with drug abuse, and this means that the levels of drug use reported by the boys in the survey might underestimate to a small extent the level of drug use within the general population of boys in schools.

Location of the schools and the pupil's homes

Sixty per cent of the informants were from schools in the Portsmouth Education Area and 40 per cent were from schools in the South East Hampshire Education Area. (Table 3.2)

Table 3.2 Survey of young people: location of pupils' schools and homes

Column percentages

School or College		
Porstmouth Education Area	60	
S.E. Hants Education Area		40
Home address		
Porstmouth local authority area	53	
Southsea		10
Central Porstmouth		21
North End		8
Cosham, Paulsgrove, Wymering, Drayton and Farlington		15
Havant local authority area	37	
Havant Town and Hayling Island		14
Leigh Park, Waterloorville, Purbrook and Cowplain		24
Other area/not stated	10	

Analysis of the age and sex breakdowns of the pupils from each area shows that the two samples were very similar in profile, with the exception that among the pupils from East Hampshire there was a larger proportion of 12-year-olds and smaller proportion of 15-year-olds. Although this is a minor difference, we mention it here because it does have a small but noticeable effect on other comparisons between the areas.

The pupils' homes were divided between the Portsmouth and Havant local authority areas in much the same way as the schools, as would be expected. The table also breaks down the pupils' home addresses into districts. It can be seen that the pupils in our sample came from a wide range of districts throughout the Portsmouth and Havant area. The information was obtained by giving the pupils a list of districts, with a map, and asking them to indicate where they lived; the actual question can be seen on the questionnaire in the appendix. One in ten ticked the 'other' category. Over half of them were aged 16 to 19, and probably did live outside the area; as for the rest of the 'others', it is likely that a number of them lived in the Portsmouth and Havant area but had difficulty identifying their district within our list, so the proportion actually living outside the area was probably smaller than the table suggests.

Parents' work

About one in ten of the pupils' fathers were not in paid work. (Table 3.3). We do not have any more details: most of them were likely to be unemployed, but a small proportion may have retired, or were not working as a result of sickness or disability. Nearly a third of the pupils' mothers were not in paid work. Again, we do not know the reason, and we cannot therefore judge how many were unemployed and how many were keeping house.

The proportion out of work was higher for the Portsmouth fathers than for the Havant fathers. It is difficult to tell from other sources what the actual unemployment rate is in the two towns, but comparisons of the 1981 Census and recent Department of Employment statistics suggest that over the last six years unemployment has grown faster in

Portsmouth than in Havant, suggesting that the survey results reflect a real difference between the areas.

Table 3.3 Survey of young people: occupation of father and mother

Column percentages

Father		
In paid work	88	
Manual		44
Non-manual		26
Work not classified		17
Not in paid work	11	
Mother		
In paid work	69	
Manual		38
Non-manual		26
Work not classified		5
Not in paid work	30	

We attempted to classify the jobs into manual and non-manual categories, but in a substantial number of cases (20 per cent of the working fathers and seven per cent of the working mothers) the description given was inadequate and their occupation appears in the table as 'not classified'. The occupational data therefore have to be treated with caution. For fathers, 63 per cent of the classified jobs were manual, and the corresponding figure for mothers was 59 per cent. It is interesting to note that among fathers the proportion of manual workers was higher in Portsmouth than in Havant (71 per cent as opposed to 59 per cent); the 1981 Census confirms that the proportion of manual workers is higher in Portsmouth. Among mothers also there was a difference between Portsmouth and Havant, but the figures are closer together.

Leisure, life-style and self-image

Leisure

We presented the pupils with a list of leisure activities and asked them to tick the ones they had done or participated in. Table 3.4 shows the results, with the most popular activities at the top of the list and the least popular at the bottom.

Table 3.4 Survey of young people: activities outside school in last seven days

Column percentages

	All	Male	Female	11	16-19
Watch TV	98	98	97	97	99
Listen to records	92	91	93	82	97
Listen to radio	78	77	79	67	88
Read a book	65	59	70	76	61
Play sport	59	75	46	65	49
Play board games	53	58	49	66	38
Draw or paint	51	52	50	72	32
Go out with family	51	49	52	60	40
Watch video	44	50	38	38	42
Go to youth club	30	34	27	45	12
Go to cinema/theatre	28	30	26	35	25
Go to pub	27	29	26	12	56
Go to party	26	24	28	19	35
Play a musical instrument	23	21	25	31	22
Work on car/bicycle	23	39	10	18	21
Go to church	17	15	18	21	22
Do voluntary work	11	10	13	13	9
TOTAL (100%)	1,063	483	579	141	227

Note: the figures for the 11-year-olds and the 16-19-year-olds are shown to illustrate the extent to which leisure patterns are related to age; the age groups in between have been omitted from the table for the sake of clarity.

Nearly all the informants had watched television at home during the previous week. More than nine out of ten had listened to records, and more than seven out of ten to the radio. Two-thirds had read a book. Over half had participated in sport, played board games, drawn or painted, or gone out with their family. Nearly a half had watched a video. Over a quarter had gone to a youth club or a uniformed youth organisation, a cinema, a pub or a party. Less than a quarter had played a musical instrument, worked on a vehicle, gone to church or religious classes, or done voluntary work.

Boys were more likely than girls to have taken part in sports and to have worked on vehicles. Compared with younger pupils, older pupils were more likely to have gone to pubs and parties, and listened to records and the radio; they were less likely to have been to youth clubs, taken part in sport, played board games, drawn or painted, and gone out with their family.

Coming home

Table 3.5 shows the time each pupil said they were expected home the last time they went out in the evening without their parents. Over ten per cent did not answer the question, either because they were not given a specific time or perhaps because they did not understand the question. The times given by the others varied greatly with age, as would be expected. The majority of 11-year-olds had to be home by nine; the majority of 12 and 13-year-olds by ten; and the majority of 14 and 15-year-olds by eleven. However, a substantial minority of 14 and 15-year-olds (25 per cent) were not expected back before eleven, or were not given a time. The majority of 16 to 19-year-olds did not have to be home till after midnight, or were not given a time.

Table 3.5 Survey of young people: time expected home

Column percentages

	All	11	12,13	14,15	16-19
Don't go out on own	1	1	1	*	1
Picked up by parents	3	4	4	3	2
By 8	15	35	28	2	1
By 9	11	23	19	7	-
By 10	18	14	23	25	4
By 11	15	3	10	27	13
By 12	9	1	3	13	16
Later	5	-	1	3	17
Parents didn't say	11	-	2	9	32
No answer	12	19	9	11	14
TOTAL (100%)	1,063	141	351	344	227

Agreement and disagreement with parents

As a measure of how much discord the pupils perceived between themselves and their parents, we asked whether they agreed or disagreed about a set of subjects, and these are shown in Table 3.6. In each case we gave informants the option of saying they never discussed the subject.

For each subject, pupils who agreed with their parents overwhelmingly outnumbered those who disagreed. The only subjects that generated disagreement in a significant number of cases were the way pupils spent their money (34 per cent disagreed with their parents) and the time they came home in the evening (24 per cent disagreed). In a substantial number of homes some of the subjects seemed to be avoided : religion (61 per cent ticked 'we never discuss this'), politics and the news (39 per cent), and hobbies (26 per cent). Overall, 34 per cent did not discuss boyfriends or girlfriends, although this was related strongly to age, and, interestingly, it differed between boys and girls: the figure for 11-year-olds was 47 per cent, with no difference between girls and boys, but among older pupils got the girls discussed the subject with their parents more than the boys did.

Table 3.6 Survey of young people: agreement with parents

Row percentages

	Agree	Disagree	Never discuss it
School	80	12	7
Friends	73	12	15
Politics/News	42	17	39
Boyfriends/Girlfriends	52	11	34
Religion	26	10	61
Spending money	51	34	15
Hobbies	67	5	26
Time come home	62	24	14
Leaving school/jobs (13-19 only)	74	14	7

Expectations

Three questions asked how the pupils rated their chances of obtaining qualifications, a job, and a job that was interesting (Table 3.7). The results show that just over half were optimistic about obtaining qualifications and a job, saying their chances were 'good' or 'very good', and less than five per cent felt their chances were 'poor' or 'very poor'. Some pupils realistically judged that getting any job would be easier than getting an interesting job.

The figures hardly vary between the age groups, except that the 16 to 19-year-olds seemed a little more optimistic than the others, as might be expected from a group that included many who had already been academically successful and others who were taking specifically vocational courses.

Table 3.7 Survey of young people: expectations

Column percentages

	All	11	12,13	14,15	16-19
Chances of getting qualifications I want					
Good/very good	54	50	55	51	57
Fair	39	43	39	39	35
Poor/very poor	4	3	3	7	4
Chances of getting a job					
Good/very good	53	45	52	49	66
Fair	39	45	41	43	28
Poor/very poor	4	4	5	4	3
Chances of getting an interesting job					
Good/very good	45	41	45	44	50
Fair	40	45	37	41	41
Poor/very poor	11	11	16	12	5
TOTAL (100%)	1,063	141	351	344	227

Risks

To find out how pupils perceived themselves in terms of risk-taking, we asked whether they would do each of a set of activities that were dangerous, illegal, unhealthy or generally frowned upon by parents or people in authority. Table 3.8 shows the proportions of pupils who said they would do them. Although there was a set of seven 'core risks' common to all versions of the questionnaire, there were others that only appeared on the questionnaires for specific age groups. It is very important to understand that this question did not seek to find out what the pupils had actually done, nor to predict what they were likely to do. Questions such as this are notoriously unreliable in their ability to predict actual behaviour. Rather, the aim was to see if pupils liked to see themselves as risk-takers.

Table 3.8 Survey of young people: views on risks

Column percentages

	All	Male	Female	11	12,13	14,15	16-19
Would you ever...							
Get in fight	52	63	42	54	49	59	44
Ride motorbike without helmet	22	28	18	9	17	33	22
Play cards for money	41	48	35	26	34	51	46
Accept lift from stranger	3	4	3	1	1	3	10
Play truant	34	34	35	13	15	43	65
Write graffiti	26	25	27	16	26	39	14
Steal	17	24	11	14	13	24	16
Total number ticked (mean)	2.0	2.3	1.7	1.3	1.5	2.5	2.2
11 and 12 year olds only							
Let dog lick face	42	44	40	37	45		
Go to bed without cleaning teeth	67	68	65	68	66		
Buy fireworks	17	22	11	14	18		
13-19 year olds only							
Go pot-holing, mountaineering or hang-gliding	46	54	39		45	47	42
Drive car without licence	20	26	15		14	21	23
Sixth-formers and college students only							
Avoid paying fare	33	47	25				33

The answer is that some did, but not many. For each of the activities listed, with the exceptions of getting involved in a fight and failing to clean their teeth before going to bed, a majority of pupils said they would not do it. Out of the seven core risks pupils ticked an average of two. Only 20 per cent of them ticked four or more, and over 25 per cent did not tick any.

For the activities that might reasonably be judged the most risky, the majority against was overwhelming: 97 per cent would not accept a lift with a stranger, 83 per cent said they would not steal, and 78 per cent said they would not ride on a motorcycle without a helmet. Eighty-three per cent of pupils under 14 said they would not buy fireworks and 80 per cent of older pupils said they would not drive a car without a licence. The less risky things tended to be the ones that pupils more readily admitted they would do: playing cards for money, not cleaning their teeth, letting a dog lick their face, missing a day of school or college, and avoiding paying a bus fare. There is an anomaly, however, and that is the large proportion who said they would get in a fight. Fighting is both dangerous and generally discouraged by adults but over 60 per cent of boys and over 40 per cent of girls said they would do it.

There are sex differences and they can be seen in the table. Most of them are predictable: boys were more likely than girls to say they would do most things, and in particular more of them said they would fight, steal, buy fireworks, play cards, avoid paying bus fares, and drive a car without a licence. There was a general tendency for older pupils to say yes to more risks, but the 14 and 15-year-olds scored higher than the 16 to 19-year-olds on the majority of items in the list.

Use of alcohol, tobacco and illicit drugs

Drinking

Pupils were asked whether they had ever tried an alcoholic drink, and if so, whether they had drunk alcohol during the month or week before the survey. The overwhelming majority (87 per cent) said they had tried alcohol, 64 per cent had had a drink in the previous month, and 41 per cent had had a drink in the previous week (Table 3.9). Older pupils were more likely than younger pupils to have tried alcohol and much more likely to have done so recently. Three-quarters of the 11-year-olds had tried alcohol, compared with nearly all the 16 to 19-year-olds; 18 per cent of the younger pupils had drunk some in the week before the survey, compared with 67 per cent of the older ones. Over half of the older pupils had been in a pub in the previous week, as had nearly a fifth of the 11-year-olds.

If we treat pub-going and drinking during the previous week as indicators of regular drinking, we can conclude that the proportion of regular drinkers rose steeply between the youngest and oldest informants from about 15 per cent to over 60 per cent. When evaluating these figures it should be remembered that only five per cent of the survey informants were old enough to buy alcohol legally. The survey therefore suggests a considerable amount of under-age drinking in pubs and a large number of illegal off-sales to young people.

Comparisons of boys and girls do not show consistent differences in their use of alcohol: for example, between the ages of 12 and 15 the proportion who had tried a drink was a little higher among the girls, but the proportion who had drunk in the last week was a little higher among the boys. In the sample as a whole, the proportions of boys and girls who had had a drink in the previous week were very close, at 43 per cent and 40 per cent respectively.

Smoking

We asked about smoking by using the same questions as for alcohol; we asked only about cigarettes, and made no mention of pipes or cigars, which are rarely the choice of young smokers.

Just over half of the pupils had tried cigarettes. One in seven had smoked in the previous week (Table 3.9). As in the case of alcohol, there is a steep age gradient: nearly a quarter of 11-year-olds had tried a cigarette, but hardly any of them had smoked in the previous week; two-thirds of the 16 to 19-year-olds had tried smoking and a quarter had smoked in the previous week. The age gradient flattens out earlier than it does with alcohol - in other words, the overall picture of tobacco use did not change very much after the age of 15 when compared with alcohol use. A third of 14 and 15-year-old pupils had not smoked, and the figure is the same for 16 to 19 year-olds; 20 per cent of the younger group had smoked in the previous week, and 24 per cent of the older group. These figures suggest that a substantial part of smoking behaviour is determined early in the teenage years.

Table 3.9 Survey of young people: alcohol and cigarettes

Column percentages

	All	11	12,13	14,15	16-19
Never tried alcohol	11	21	18	6	3
Tried alcohol	87	78	81	92	96
Had a drink in last month	64	43	50	74	85
Had a drink in last week	41	18	28	47	67
Been to a pub in last week	27	12	13	30	56
Never tried cigarettes	47	77	58	33	33
Tried cigarettes	52	23	42	66	65
Had a cigarette in last month	19	1	11	27	29
Had a cigarette in last week	14	1	5	20	24
TOTAL (100%)	1,063	141	351	344	227

Three-quarters of those who had experimented with cigarettes and over half of those who had smoked in the previous week were under 16 years old, the legal minimum age for purchasing cigarettes. It is therefore likely that most of the smokers in the sample were buying their cigarettes illegally.

As with alcohol, there were no substantial or consistent differences between girls' and boys' use of cigarettes. Overall, 12 per cent of the boys had had a cigarette in the previous week, compared with 15 per cent of the girls.

Illicit drugs

Even people who do not drink alcohol or smoke cigarettes know others who do. This is not the case for illicit drugs: most adults would say they do not know any drug users. For this reason it is important to know how many young people know drug users, in addition to how many are themselves users. In the same way as for alcohol and tobacco, the questionnaire asked pupils if they had ever taken illicit drugs and, if so, whether they had done so in the previous month and previous week. Before that, however, pupils were asked whether they knew anyone who took drugs. As well as providing important extra information, this approach provided an introduction to the sensitive questions on personal drug use. The pupils in classes in the third year (13 and 14-year-olds) and above in secondary schools were asked about the use of solvents, cannabis, heroin and amphetamine, and about any 'other drugs'. The youngest pupils were asked specifically about sniffing solvents but then only generally about all 'other drugs', which they had to specify if they knew a user or used themselves; on their forms the questions did not specifically mention cannabis, heroin or amphetamine.

The results are given in Table 3.10. The top part of the table shows the answers aggregated for all drugs except solvents, which are discussed separately later. About a third of all the pupils said they knew someone who had taken an illicit drug, and one in 20 said they had done so themselves. Like the use of alcohol and tobacco, illicit drug use is strongly related to age, so the overall figures hide a more complicated pattern. Very few of the 11-year-olds even knew any drug users, but this rose to 12 per cent of 12 and 13-year-olds, and eventually to 46 per cent of 16 to 19-year-olds. There was almost no drug use at all among the pupils aged under 14, but five per cent of the 14 and 15-year-olds had used, and this rose to 12 per cent among the 16 to 19-year-olds. It seems, therefore, that during the period of their secondary schooling, between a third and a half of pupils come into contact with someone who has used an illicit drug, and up to one in ten themselves try a drug.

It should be remembered that contact with drug users is not necessarily at school, and it could be argued that it is more likely to be at home (older brothers and sisters, or even parents) or while out with older friends. We cannot tell from this survey. Analysis of the geographical location both of those who know users and of those who have used drugs shows very little clustering in particular areas or in particular schools.

Table 3.10 Survey of young people: illicit drugs (excluding solvents)

Column percentages

	All	11	12,13	14,15	16-19
Any illicit drug					
Don't know any drug users	70	96	87	59	42
Know drug user(s) but have never used	26	4	12	36	46
Have used drug(s) ever	5	1	1	5	12
in last month	3	1	*	4	6
in last week	1	-	-	1	3
Cannabis					
Know user(s), never used	22	2	6	32	44
Have used ever	4	-	1	5	11
in last month	2	-	-	4	6
in last week	1	-	-	1	3
Amphetamine					
Know user(s), never used	11	-	3	16	26
Have used ever	1	-	-	2	3
in last month	1	-	-	1	1
in last week	*	-	-	1	-
Heroin					
Know user(s), never used	12	2	7	18	16
Have used ever	1	-	*	2	*
in last month	1	-	*	2	*
in last week	*	-	-	-	-
LSD, magic mushrooms					
Know user(s), never used	4	-	1	4	9
Have used ever	*	-	*	*	1
in last month	*	-	-	-	*
in last week	-	-	-	-	-
TOTAL (100%)	1,063	141	351	344	227

Only six per cent of pupils had used drugs in the month before the survey, and only one per cent in the week before. Among those older than 14, about one in 20 had used a drug in the last month. Only one per cent of the 14 and 15-year-olds, and three per cent of the 16 to 19-year-olds, had used in the previous week. This suggests that only a proportion of those who try drugs go on to become regular users, a smaller proportion than with tobacco and a much smaller proportion than with alcohol.

Analysis of the boys and girls separately shows that, as for tobacco and alcohol, there were no consistent differences in their knowledge of drug users or in their own use. Contrary to what might have been expected, the girls in our sample were not less likely than the boys to know users or to use themselves.

Which illicit drugs?

Separate figures are given in Table 3.10 for cannabis, amphetamine, heroin, and hallucinogens. It should be remembered that the figures for each drug are not exclusive; for example, those who knew heroin users were also quite likely to know cannabis users, and appear in both parts of the table.

(i) Cannabis

Most of the reported drug use, either by people known to the pupils or by the pupils themselves, was cannabis smoking. Two-thirds of those who had taken an illicit drug had used only cannabis. The figures for cannabis are therefore very similar to those given above for illicit drugs in general. The proportion of pupils who knew a cannabis user rose from two per cent among the youngest to 44 per cent among the oldest, and the proportion who had smoked it themselves rose from zero to 11 per cent. About five per cent of pupils aged over 14 smoked cannabis in the month before the survey; one per cent of 14 and 15-year-olds had smoked it in the previous week, and the corresponding figure for 16 to 19-year-olds was three per cent.

(ii) Amphetamine

The figures for amphetamine are much lower than for cannabis. Hardly any pupils under 14 knew anyone who had used it, and none had used themselves. Among older pupils, only about two to three per cent had tried amphetamine, and less than one per cent said they had used in the last week.

The contrast with cannabis is interesting, since amphetamine is thought by some to be almost as widely used among young people as is cannabis. The explanation could be that amphetamine use becomes much more widespread among those who have left school, and 'catches up' with cannabis; alternatively, it could be that cannabis use is in fact more common than amphetamine use among all age groups. Two-thirds of the pupils who had used amphetamines had also used cannabis.

(iii) Heroin

The figures for heroin are very low, and are similar to those for amphetamine. Up to the age of 13, less than five per cent knew anyone who had used it, and only one pupil claimed to have used it - less than half of one per cent. About 15 per cent of all the older pupils knew someone who had used heroin, and about one per cent had used it. One per cent of those over 13 said they had used heroin in the last month, and less than one per cent said they had done so in the last week. In total there were only nine pupils in the survey who said they had used heroin. It is interesting to note that those who knew users and those who had used came more from the 14 and 15-year-old group than from the oldest group, and this was not the case for any other drugs.

Eight out of the nine pupils who had used heroin had also used cannabis, and three had used amphetamine.

(iv) LSD and 'magic mushrooms'

The numbers for hallucinogenic drugs are even lower than for heroin. None of the 11-year-olds said they knew anyone who took LSD or magic mushrooms, and the proportion rose to only nine per cent among the oldest pupils. Only five pupils claimed to have had personal experience of such a drug, and only one was in the last month.

(v) Other illicit drugs

A very small number of pupils (fewer than ten) said they had used or knew someone who had used drugs other than those listed above; most were talking about other people and not their own use. These were mostly sedatives and tranquillisers, although two pupils mentioned amyl nitrite ('poppers'), which is not an controlled drug, and two mentioned 'angel dust' and 'rainbow dust' (PCP).

Drug use by drinkers and smokers

The use of illicit drugs was more common among drinkers and smokers than among other pupils. Table 3.11 shows the drug behaviour of those who drank and those who smoked during the week before the survey. Comparing first the drinkers and non-drinkers, we can see that in the sample as a whole the drinkers were much more likely to know drug users and to have used themselves. Although some of the relationship is the result of the age differences within the sample, some association persists if we look at the older age groups on their own: the proportion of drug users among the drinkers is twice as high as among the non-drinkers, and the proportion who knew drug users is about one-and-a-half times higher. More than 80 per cent of drug users had had a drink in the previous week; this compares with just over half of the other older pupils.

Comparing smokers and non-smokers, we see the same type of differences but they are much larger. Smokers were a smaller group than drinkers, and a substantial proportion of them knew illicit drug users and had used themselves. The table reveals that nearly three-quarters of the smokers in the sample knew someone who had used drugs, compared with only a quarter of non-smokers. Even more striking is the finding that a quarter of all the smokers had tried an illicit drug, compared with only one per cent of the non-smokers. Again, there is some reflection of the sample's wide age range in the differing proportions of smokers and non-smokers who knew drug users. But even when we look at the older age groups on their own most of the relationship remains, and the association between smoking and drug use by the individual pupil remains as strong.

It is important to note that this strong association between smoking and drug use does not necessarily imply causation. It is feasible that smoking is the first step along the path to illicit drug use, but it is equally feasible that pupils who try illicit drugs also take up smoking as part of their general abuse of drugs. Given that most of the pupils who had used drugs were in the older age groups, perhaps the best way to state the findings of the survey is to compare the smoking habits of the drug users with those of other older pupils: 76 per cent of the drug users were smokers, compared with only 17 per cent of the rest.

Table 3.11 Survey of young people: drug use by smokers and drinkers

Column percentages

	No drink last week	Drink last week	No cigarette last week	Cigarette last week
All				
Don't know drug users	80	53	76	28
Know drug user(s) but never used	18	38	23	45
Have used drug(s)	2	9	1	26
TOTAL (100%)	601	436	897	145
Age 14-15				
Don't know drug users	67	48	68	27
Know drug user(s) but never used	31	43	31	51
Have used drug(s)	2	9	1	21
TOTAL (100%)	175	160	263	70
Age 16-19				
Don't know drug users	52	36	48	18
Know drug user(s) but never used	41	49	48	46
Have used drug(s)	7	15	4	36
TOTAL (100%)	152	71	166	55

Characteristics of drinkers, smokers and illicit drug users

The survey was designed to find out whether the pupils who used tobacco, alcohol and illicit drugs were different in any way from the rest. To do this we systematically tabulated the answers to all the questions for users and non-users of each drug. Many differences emerged from this analysis, most of which are in the direction that one would expect, although some are surprising. The results given below show the more important and interesting relationships.

Drinkers and smokers

For the purpose of this analysis, shown in Tables 3.12 and 3.13, we have again defined alcohol and tobacco users as those who had had a drink or a cigarette during the previous week.

(i) Parents' occupation

Overall, the proportion of pupils' fathers who were not employed was slightly lower among drinkers and smokers than among others. The same was true for pupils' mothers. Although these are not particularly strong relationships, they are perhaps a little surprising: they serve to show that in Portsmouth and Havant under-age drinking and smoking are not associated with the disadvantage of parental unemployment.

As explained earlier in the report, it is difficult to use the information on the actual jobs done by parents because of the quality of the answers given on the forms. Using a simple split between manual and non-manual jobs, we cannot see any consistent relationships between parents' occupation and pupils' smoking and drinking.

(ii) Time expected home

Overall, the pupils who did not drink and smoke had to be home early, but that was largely a product of the age difference. In the older age groups there was no consistent relationship with smoking. However, the proportion of older pupils who had to be home before 11 is higher among those who did not drink the previous week.

(iii) Pocket money and earned money

One might expect pupils' alcohol and tobacco behaviour to be strongly related to the amount of money they earn or are given, but this was not the case. Once age is taken into account, there was no difference between the amounts of pocket money received by users of alcohol and cigarettes and those received by the other pupils. As for earned money, some smokers and drinkers earned more than others, but there was very little difference between them.

Ta ble 3.12 Survey of young people: characteristics of drinkers

Column percentages

	All		12,13		14,15		16-19	
	Users	Non Users	Users	Non-Users	Users	Non-Users	Users	Non - Users
Father not employed	7	14	1	13	6	21	4	11
Mother not employed	23	35	32	35	18	33	23	37
Expected home by 11	49	75	82	86	54	74	16	32
Last week								
Been to a pub	51	10	29	5	49	13	72	23
Been to a party	38	17	26	16	44	17	41	21
Would you ever ...								
Get in fight	60	47	60	45	66	54	51	31
Ride motorbike without helmet	32	16	26	14	41	27	27	13
Play cards for money	56	32	50	28	64	42	51	37
Accept lift from stranger	6	2	3	-	3	2	11	7
Play truant	49	25	18	13	52	37	69	59
Write graffiti	32	23	33	24	48	33	15	13
Steal	22	14	18	10	31	19	16	17
Buy fireworks			29	15				
Go pot-holing, mountaineering or hang-gliding					59	39	56	46
Drive car without licence					29	14	23	18
Avoid paying fare							40	21
Mean number of core risks	2.6	1.6	2.1	1.3	3.0	2.1	2.4	1.8
TOTAL (100%)	436	601	98	244	160	175	152	71

Ta ble 3.13 Survey of young people: characteristics of smokers

Column percentages

	All		14,15		16-19	
	Users	Non Users	Users	Non-Users	Users	Non-Users
Father not employed	10	12	11	16	6	7
Mother not employed	27	31	26	26	24	29
Expected home by 11	48	67	56	67	24	20
Last week						
Read book	46	68	40	60	47	66
Went out with family	35	54	36	52	24	45
Been to a pub	51	23	50	24	76	50
Been to a party	44	23	43	27	51	30
Would you ever ...						
Get in fight	70	49	74	56	64	39
Ride motorbike without helmet	50	18	57	27	38	17
Play cards for money	60	38	63	48	56	43
Accept lift from stranger	8	3	4	2	13	9
Play truant	69	29	74	35	73	64
Write graffiti	51	23	63	33	27	10
Steal	37	14	44	19	27	13
Go pot-holing, mountaineering or hang-gliding			49	48	42	57
Drive car without licence			34	17	29	15
Avoid paying fare					34	33
Mean number of core risks	3.4	1.7	3.0	2.2	3.0	1.9
TOTAL (100%)	145	897	70	263	55	166

(iv) Leisure activities in the past week

There were differences between the leisure activities of drinkers and the rest, but most of them were small, and they became smaller once age was taken into account: for example, during the previous week a slightly larger proportion of drinkers listened to the radio (85 per cent compared with 74 per cent) and a slightly smaller proportion did some painting or drawing (44 per cent compared with 57 per cent). The only substantial differences concerned pubs and party-going, and they were as expected: half the drinkers went to a pub and over a third went to a party, much higher proportions than for those who did not drink the previous week. It should be noted that over a quarter of 12 and 13 year-olds, and half the 14 and 15-year-olds, seemed to have done their drinking in a pub.

Smokers listed pubs and parties among their leisure activities more commonly than non-smokers, although the difference was not as great as that between drinkers and non-drinkers (few pupils went to a pub or party without having an alcoholic drink, but the majority did so without smoking). Smokers were less likely than non-smokers to have been out with their family, or to have read a book. As in the case of alcohol, there are other minor differences between smokers and non-smokers which were too small to show on the table.

(v) Risks

Relatively large proportions of both drinkers and smokers said they would take the risks listed on the questionnaire. The average number of 'core risks' that drinkers said they would take is 2.6, compared with 1.6 for non-drinkers; for smokers and non-smokers, the figures are 3.4 and 1.7 respectively. Age plays some part in this, since older pupils admitted to more risks, but even among the older pupils there was still a substantial gap between the users and non-users, and it was wider for smoking than it for drinking.

Although the table does not show girls and boys separately, further analysis reveals that the relationship between perceived risk-taking and the use of alcohol and tobacco exists for both sexes. In some ways the relationships are shown to be stronger: for example, on the table the figures for mountaineering and potholing seem to go against the trend (for smokers), but once the girls and boys are separated, the pattern falls in with the rest.

(vi) Agreement and disagreement with parents

There was a minor current of disagreement running through the replies of the drinkers and smokers, but it was not important enough to include in the table. At the most it indicates that the minority of pupils who said they disagreed with their parents about each subject (and those who never discussed it) is slightly larger among the drinkers and smokers.

(vii) Expectations

Drinkers and smokers do not stand out from the rest of the pupils in respect of their exam or employment expectations.

Illicit drugs

For the analysis of illicit drug use we split the sample into those who had ever used and those who had not. This is a different definition of a 'user' from the one used for alcohol and tobacco, for which we split the sample according to use in the previous week. Further, we divided the pupils who had never taken illicit drugs into those who knew a user and those who did not. The aim of this three-way division was to see how far the users differed from those who had encountered drugs, if only in a limited way, but had never taken them. The user group is much smaller than the 'knowing' group, and it is of some importance to know the characteristics of those who did take up the opportunity to use drugs and those who did not. In fact, as Table 3.14 shows, the pattern is simple: on most of the characteristics, the pupils who only knew users fell in between the users and the rest.

(i) Parents' occupation

Hardly any of the drug users had unemployed fathers, and the proportion whose mothers did not go out to work is lower than among non-users. Like the use of tobacco and alcohol, then, we see that pupils' illicit drug use cannot be associated with parental unemployment. Analysis of the actual jobs suggests that drug users tended to have parents in non-manual work more often than pupils who had never tried drugs, although this is not a strong relationship.

Table 3.14 Survey of young people: characteristics of drug users and those who know drug users

	All			14,15			16-19		
	Don't know users	Know users	User	Don't know users	Know users	User	Don't know users	Know users	User
Father not employed	12	10	2	16	13	6	10	4	-
Mother not employed	30	32	16	25	31	6	28	29	22
Expected home by 11	72	48	24	69	62	21	30	15	15
Last week									
Read book	68	61	43	60	53	28	63	64	48
Play board game	57	47	22	54	50	28	41	41	19
Went out with family	57	41	20	55	42	22	50	35	22
Watch video	41	46	67	45	53	89	46	36	56
To cinema/theatre	28	26	43	25	30	44	27	18	44
To pub	18	43	80	22	38	78	40	63	89
To party	21	33	57	24	36	61	28	36	56
Would you ever ...									
Get in fight	47	60	69	51	67	94	33	50	56
Ride motorbike without helmet	15	37	51	20	49	72	16	24	37
Play cards for money	34	55	65	44	58	83	35	53	56
Accept lift from stranger	1	7	18	1	3	22	4	14	15
Play truant	22	58	80	30	59	78	51	72	85
Write graffiti	21	35	59	27	54	78	7	14	44
Steal	12	27	45	16	32	67	10	17	30
Go pot-holing, mountaineering or hang-gliding				43	55	44	44	62	44
Drive car without licence				10	31	72	8	38	44
Avoid paying fare							23	38	43
Mean number of core risks	1.5	2.8	3.9	1.9	3.2	4.9	1.6	2.4	3.2
TOTAL (100%)	740	274	49	204	122	18	96	104	27

(ii) Time expected home

The proportion of pupils who had to be home before 11 o'clock was larger for non-users than it was for users, even among the older age groups.

(iii) Pocket money and earned money

There was hardly any difference in the levels of pocket money or earned money between users and non-users. There was no difference in the proportions who received any pocket money or in the proportions who earned money themselves; the average sums of money were higher for users, but only a little. The results for cigarettes and alcohol were almost the same.

(iv) Leisure activities in the past week

Users were more likely than others to have been to pubs, parties and the cinema or the theatre. They were more also likely to have watched a video. They were less likely than others to have gone out with their family, read a book, or played chess, draughts or other board games. All these relationships stand up to examination in individual age groups, so they are not just functions of the fact that users tended to be older, and they are all quite strong.

There were, as for alcohol and tobacco, a number of minor additional differences between the leisure patterns of users and non-users, and these are not shown on the table. Users were slightly less likely to have taken part in sport or worked on a bicycle, motorcycle or car; and they were slightly more likely to have done some drawing or painting.

(v) Risks

The drug users were very distinct from the rest of the pupils in their answers to the questions on risks. For nearly every risky activity on the list, a far higher proportion of users said they would do it. We do not know whether or not they really would take those risks, but the illicit drug users did wish to see themselves as the sort of people who would.

The average numbers of 'core risks' ticked by users, those who only knew users, and those who did not know users are 3.9, 2.8 and 1.5 respectively. As can be seen in the table, this relationship does not break down when the older age groups are considered separately. A majority of illicit drug users said they would get into a fight, play cards for money, miss a day of school or college, write or spray graffiti on a wall, and drive without a licence. About half said they would ride a motorbike without a helmet, and steal. All these proportions are very much higher than for non-users. Eighteen per cent of drug users said they would accept a lift from a stranger, compared with only one per cent of those who did not know users. For all these items, the pupils who only knew users fall more or less mid-way between the users and the pupils who did not know any users.

The dangerous sports item is an exception, perhaps a revealing one. The illicit drug users were no more likely than the others to say they would go mountaineering or pot-holing; the pupils who only knew users ticked this item most frequently. Perhaps the reason is that the type of risk that it represents is different from the others. Most of the other items in the list (for older pupils) are risky because they are illegal or frowned upon by parents and figures of authority: they are sleazy. Riding without a crash helmet, accepting lifts from strangers and fighting are physically dangerous, but they also fall into the category of things you would not admit to your mother. Mountaineering and pot-holing are both physically dangerous - the newspapers usually report the accidents with as much relish as they do drug scandals - but they are held in heroic esteem in our society. Teachers, youth leaders, police officers and scoutmasters all agree that risk-taking like this is character-building; it has official sanction, and therefore, despite its obvious danger, it loses some of the rebellious glamour that it might have were it condemned as reckless and irresponsible.

(vi) Agreement and disagreement with parents

There were minor differences between the drug users and the others in respect of the proportions who disagreed with their parents over the subjects listed on the questionnaire. The patterns are like those for alcohol and tobacco - the users were slightly more likely to say they disagreed (or say they did not discuss the subject) with their parents.

(vii) Expectations
Some of the pupils who had used drugs were more pessimistic about their exam and job prospects than those who had not, but there was not a big difference.

Heroin users
Most of the drug users described in the above analysis were cannabis users. After the publicity that heroin has attracted over the past five years, however, it is natural that there was some interest in the pupils who admitted to having used heroin.

There were nine pupils who said they had used heroin, and a majority said they had used it in the last month. Four were girls and five were boys. Seven were in the 14 and 15-year-old group, one was 13 and another was 17. Five of them lived in Portsmouth, three lived in the Havant area, and one lived elsewhere in the county.

All of the heroin users' mothers and fathers went out to work. In general, the heroin users were not very different from the rest of the illicit drug users, except in their answers to the risk questions, which suggest that most of them were stereotype drug users: seven of them ticked five or more of the core risks.

Solvent abuse
The questionnaire treated solvents as a drug in just the same way as cannabis and heroin. Pupils were asked whether they knew anyone who sniffed them and whether they had done so themselves.

Solvents are the only substances covered by the survey that are not subject to legal controls and with which everyone has had a small amount of experience, however unintentional. This leads to a real difficulty of interpretation. We are not convinced that the sniffing reported in the survey was in all cases sniffing that leads to intoxication. Pupils, aware of the media alarm and parental concern over this issue, may have felt some guilt about their experimental sniffing of the glue or cleaning fluids kept in their own homes - and reported it in the survey as solvent sniffing. In other words, the survey results probably overestimate the extent of abuse; among the pupils who said they had sniffed solvents there must have been some who were abusers, but we cannot say how many.

The reported level of glue and solvent sniffing was, compared with other drugs, fairly high for the younger pupils in the survey. As they stand, the figures suggest that over four per cent of all pupils had tried solvent sniffing; among 11 year-olds it was over seven per cent. Over two per cent of pupils claimed to have done it in the last month. About 25 per cent said they knew someone who had sniffed solvents; it is interesting to note that this figure rises with age, from 15 per cent among the youngest to 33 per cent among the oldest, and this is in sharp contrast to the trend for reported personal use, which was more prevalent among younger pupils.

The methodological problem of disentangling solvent abuse from less sinister contacts with solvents is not merely a technical one. In an interview survey it would be easy to add follow-up questions for clarification. However, with a short, self-completion questionnaire, there is a difficulty: it would be possible to ask a more detailed question such as 'Have you ever sniffed glue, cleaning fluids or other substances, on purpose, to make yourself feel and act drunk?', but that would be likely to put the idea of solvent abuse into an innocent pupil's mind. Given that one of the general worries of carrying out this kind of survey is the possibility of arousing interest in drug use, particular care is needed over the repercussions of individual questions. We worded this question 'on the safe side', which was probably the right thing to do, but the price has been the loss of some of the question's accuracy.

Comparisons with other surveys

Surprisingly few surveys of drug use have been conducted in Britain, and there is therefore a limited number of sources of comparison for the results of this survey. The Portsmouth and Havant survey results are, however, closely in line with the others.

Two fairly recent national studies provide comparisons, one for cannabis and the other for alcohol. The first is the 1982 National Crime Survey (BCS), sponsored by the Home Office, and the second is the survey of young people's drinking habits conducted by the Office of Population Censuses and Surveys (OPCS). Both were self-report surveys, like our own, but they differed considerably in the way that they were carried out. The results of both are shown in Table 3.15.

Table 3.15 Survey of young people: comparisons with other surveys

(i) British Crime Survey (BCS)

	Per cent ever used cannabis	
	Male	Female
BCS (1982):		
Aged 16-19, still in education	8	3
All aged 16-19	10	6
PSI Survey (1986/7):		
Pupils aged 16-19	11	12

(ii) OPCS Survey of Adolescent Drinking

Column percentages

	Male			Female		
	13	14	15	13	14	15
OPCS (1984):						
Never tasted acohol	6	3	2	7	4	2
Never had a 'proper' drink	18	22	8	24	13	9
PSI Survey (1986/7):						
Never tried an alcoholic drink	20	11	9	11	7	-
Had a drink last week						
OPCS	34	40	60	30	45	56
PSI	31	43	53	32	33	56

(iii) Lothian Survey

Column percentages

	Male	Female
Lothian (1979/80):		
(15 and 16-year-olds)		
Never tasted an acoholic drink	2	2
Had a drink last week	44	31
Have ever tried an illicit drug (including solvents)	15	11
Have tried:		
Cannabis	7	7
Amphetamine	2	3
Heroin	1	0.4
Glue/solvents	5	4
Portsmouth/Havant (1986/7):		
(15 and 16-year-olds)		
Never tasted an acoholic drink	6	3
Had a drink last week	61	60
Have ever tried an illicit drug (including solvents)	14	9
Have tried:		
Cannabis	11	8
Amphetamine	2	3
Heroin	2	2
Glue/solvents	6	2

Looking first at the cannabis figures, we can see that the proportion of Portsmouth and Havant pupils aged 16 to 19 who said they had used it was rather higher than for 16 to 19-year-old pupils in the BCS survey, particularly in the case of girls. The BCS figure for all 16 to 19-year-olds, including those who had left school or college, are closer to the PSI figures: taking boys and girls together, both surveys give a figure near to ten per cent.

The comparison between the PSI figures and the OPCS figures for alcohol is more complicated. We asked pupils whether they had ever 'tried an alcoholic drink'. The OPCS survey was more sophisticated, making a distinction between 'never tasted alcohol' and 'never had a proper drink'. The PSI figures for boys match closely the OPCS 'proper drink' figures for boys, while the PSI figures for girls are nearer to the OPCS 'never tasted' figures. This difference between the boys and girls is fascinating, because it suggests that perhaps they did not interpret 'trying a drink' in the same way: if the OPCS figures are a correct benchmark, the boys tended to interpret the PSI question as referring to a 'proper drink' while the girls tended to interpret it as referring to a sip of someone else's, or perhaps a small glass of something at Christmas or another festive occasion. Comparisons of the proportions who had had a drink during the last week show the PSI and OPCS surveys to be very close, and this in turn suggests two things. The first is that the boys really did interpret the PSI question differently from girls (otherwise the two surveys would be unlikely to agree over consumption of alcohol in the previous week), and the second is that in the Portsmouth and Havant area the consumption of alcohol by school pupils was on a par with consumption nationally.

A study by Plant, Peck and Samuel in the Lothian Region in Scotland in the early 1980s followed teenagers over the period of their leaving school. Before leaving (when 15 or 16 years old), seven per cent had used cannabis, about three per cent had used amphetamine, under one per cent had used heroin, and about five per cent had used solvents. These figures are very close to the PSI figures for pupils of the same age in Portsmouth and Havant. Only two per cent of the Lothian pupils (at that age) had never had an alcoholic drink - rather lower than our six per cent. The proportion who had had a drink in the previous week was, however, not as high as in the PSI survey: only 44 per cent of boys and 31 per cent of girls in Lothian, compared with over 60 per cent of both in Portsmouth and Havant.

A very small survey of Portsmouth fourth-form pupils was carried out by a student at the University of Newcastle in 1985. It was part of a larger survey covering three areas of the country, and included only 30 pupils from this area. The small size of the sample (along with some other problems of the consistency of the informants' answers) makes comparison with the present survey of limited value. However, the prevalence of drug use was of a similar order as that found by the PSI survey: ten per cent (three pupils) said they had used illicit drugs other than solvents.

The other local survey is more important. Colin Pritchard and his colleagues at Southampton University carried out a survey of 807 fourth and fifth year comprehensive pupils in Bournemouth and Southampton in 1985. Their research design was an influence on our own, particularly with regard to the questionnaire. They found that just under one per cent of pupils had used heroin and ten per cent had used cannabis. The heroin figure is close to our own, but the figure for cannabis is a little higher than for the corresponding age group in our survey. There are other similarities in the more detailed analysis of Pritchard's survey: associations between drug use and smoking, drinking, truanting, fighting and vandalism echo our own findings regarding cigarettes, alcohol and risks. However, there was one finding that was different from ours: the drug users in Bournemouth and Southampton were more likely than others to have unemployed fathers, and this did not seem to be true in Portsmouth and Havant.

Assessing the extent of local drug use

Although the results as we have presented them are useful, the reader may wish to know what the percentages might mean in terms of actual numbers of local school pupils. As far as illicit drugs are concerned, the numbers obtained by making such projections are not high, and give no reason to believe that there is a drugs 'epidemic' in schools in Portsmouth and Havant.

Reasons to be careful

Projections based on survey data on drug use should be treated with a great deal of caution, and we outline below the most important points that should be borne in mind when using the survey figures.

There are three ways in which the survey percentages might be misleading when applied to the local population figures for school pupils. First, any sample survey will have a degree of possible error because it is based on a sample and not on a census of the whole population concerned. Secondly, the answers given by the pupils in the survey might not be truthful. Thirdly, the sample excludes pupils who were absent through illness or truancy, and those pupils withdrawn from the survey by their parents.

The size of the sampling error depends largely on the size and structure of the sample. If we had obtained information from nearly all the pupils in the area by giving out over 25 thousand questionnaires, this error would be almost eliminated. But our sample of 1,063 is of a respectable size, and the possible error is not as large as might be expected. For example, when a random sample of 1,063 gives a figure of one per cent who have used heroin, the mathematics of probability tell us that there is a 95 per cent chance that the true proportion of heroin users in the population is between 0.4 and 1.6 per cent; similarly, when the survey figure for cannabis use is four per cent, there is a 95 per cent chance that the true figure in the population from which the sample is drawn is between 3.4 and 4.6 per cent. The examples given here are the actual figures from the survey. For figures based on sub-groups within the survey, the possible error is larger than this, because the sub-groups are smaller than the total sample; for example, the true figure for cannabis among 14 to 19-year-olds has a range of error of about four per cent because the sample contains only 571 people in this age range, and therefore can be said to be between five and nine per cent. In fact the sampling errors for this survey will be a little higher than these figures suggest, because the pupils were sampled in batches (whole classes from selected schools) and not from a single list of all school pupils in the area; sampling in batches increases the sampling error, but the size of this increase is offset by the careful selection of schools and classes to represent different areas, age groups and abilities.

We cannot tell for certain that the pupils' answers to the questions were truthful and accurate, but the figures are largely consistent with other surveys and there are no contradictions or suspicious patterns within the results of the survey. On the contrary, the pattern of responses gives many indications that the pupils answered sensibly and honestly. The most important indications come from the differences between the numbers who said they had taken the different illegal drugs. If pupils were not admitting heroin use because they were afraid that teachers or parents would somehow find out, then why did a relatively large number (over 40) readily admit to having tried cannabis? Conversely, if pupils were showing off by ticking drugs that they had not in fact tried, then why did so few tick heroin or amphetamine? In other words, the patterns of results are not the ones that we would expect to find if there had been a significant tendency either to hide drug use or to overstate it. It should also be remembered that the conditions under which the survey was administered made it obvious to pupils that they could not be 'found out' as a result of admitting illicit drug use on the questionnaire: no names were on the forms and the PSI researchers took them away sealed in individual unmarked envelopes without the teachers seeing them.

The effect of the loss from the sample of absentees and the pupils withdrawn by parents is difficult to evaluate. Few pupils were withdrawn by parents, but we noted earlier that the absence of some boys for other reasons had a small effect on the sex ratio in the sample. It is possible that there is an association between truancy and drug-related behaviour, and if this is the case then the figures for drug use obtained from the survey will be underestimates. However, it is unlikely that this factor could had a large effect. For example, if all the absent boys and girls were truants, and if truants were four times as likely as other pupils to has taken illicit drugs, then the overall percentage of pupils who had used an illicit drug would be six per cent, rather than the five per cent shown in the survey; the equivalent calculation for the 16 to 19-year-old group on their own would put their figure at 15 per cent as opposed to the 12 per cent shown in the survey. When applied to the figures for heroin, the adjustment has almost no effect. Thus we can see that the survey figures are unlikely to be seriously biased by the absence of these pupils.

Projections

The projections given here are simple applications of the survey percentages to the local school population, and should only be cited in conjunction with the cautions given above. In Portsmouth and Havant there was in 1987 a total of about 4,100 children in each year group within the population, according to calculations based on updating the 1981 Census figures. Up to and including the age of 15 all of the children attended schools, but from the age of 16 onwards a rising proportion had left school. Overall, about 35 per cent of people aged

16 to 19 were at school or in further education; this means that in total there were about 26,000 pupils and students aged 11 to 19 in the area, and it is about this group that the survey gives us information. Note that this group excludes students in higher education.

We can assume with some confidence that hardly any children under 14 in the area had taken heroin. About one in twenty knew someone who had tried heroin (or knew someone who said so), but only one of our sample of 492 pupils in this age group claimed to have taken it herself. Among the older pupils, however, nearly one in five knew someone who had taken heroin, and 1.5 per cent had taken it themselves. If we make a projection from the results of this survey, about 170 local pupils between the ages of 14 and 16 had tried heroin, and a further 50 aged 17 to 19, making a total of 270 in the school and college population.

The projections for cannabis are much higher. For the whole 14 to 19 group in schools and further education, our figures suggest that over 1,100 had tried it, out of a total of about 15,000 pupils. This is one illustration of the widespread use of cannabis today. By comparison, few teenagers appeared to have used amphetamine: none of the under-14s, and only just over 2 per cent of the 14 to 19 year-olds, which multiplies up to about 325 in that age group.

LSD and 'magic mushrooms' had been taken by less than one per cent of pupils. None of the 11 year-olds claim to had taken hallucinogens, but half of one per cent of older pupils said they had. If this percentage is projected into the whole school and college population aged 12 to 19, the total figure is about 115.

So far these projections concern all pupils who had tried drugs, and some of them may have tried them only once. Less than two-thirds of the survey informants who had tried illicit drugs had used them during the last month. This proportion varies between drugs in the survey, but the raw numbers are so small that there is not a lot to be made of this variation. Overall, about a quarter of those who had tried drugs had taken something in the last week; of the nine pupils who had tried heroin, two used some the previous week. So, whilst we can make projections of hundreds of pupils who had tried drugs, the number of very recent users is likely to be less than a quarter of the figures we have given so far.

Not all of those who were very recent users would be regular users, so the number of regular weekly users would be smaller still. We could tentatively suggest a total weekly user population among the 14 to 19-year-old pupils of a maximum of 50 heroin users, 300 cannabis users and 70 amphetamine users. These groups overlap, in other words most heroin users and amphetamine users also used cannabis, so by adding them together we arrive at a total of less than 350 pupils. Among a group of 50 weekly heroin users, a proportion would be casual users, probably taking some during the weekend, while others would be using more frequently and some could be classed as dependent. These projections therefore suggest that there were fewer than 50 pupils dependent on heroin in Portsmouth and Havant. It should be remembered that this is out of a total school and college population of over 26,000 aged between 11 and 19.

Conclusions

The survey has provided two types of information. It has given us data on the prevalence of drug use: an idea of the numbers of pupils who have used alcohol, tobacco and illicit drugs, and an idea of the numbers who are currently doing so. It has also given us data on the ties between drug use and other features of pupils' lives: we have seen how different background factors, leisure patterns and attitudes relate to the consumption of alcohol, tobacco and illicit drugs.

Prevalence

We regard the prevalence data on cigarettes and alcohol as far more alarming than the data on illicit drugs. Tobacco and alcohol are legal drugs, but they are legally controlled and a large element of that control is intended to restrict their consumption by young people. The survey shows that over a third of pupils under the age of 18 had had an alcoholic drink in the last week, and about a quarter of pupils under 18 had been in a pub in the last week. Over a fifth of pupils aged over 14 had smoked in the last week, and more than a third of the younger pupils had at some time tried a cigarette. These figures all point to widespread under-age use of tobacco and alcohol.

We do not need to rehearse the arguments for restricting young teenagers' access to these drugs, but we should perhaps underline the argument about alcohol from a health angle: too often the issue of under-age drinking is seen only as one of bad behaviour, vandalism and public order, and this view disregards the real health hazards of long-term drinking. Damage to health as a result of drinking regularly is not restricted to those people classed as alcoholics, and many people exceed the medically safe level of alcohol consumption without realising it. Regular drinking that begins in the early teens may create serious health problems later.

In contrast to the high percentages for alcohol and tobacco, the figures for the use of illicit drugs are relatively small. Only one in twenty pupils in the survey had ever taken an illicit drug. The proportion was negligible among the 11 and 12-year-olds, and rose to 12 per cent among the 16 to 19-year-olds. The figures for recent use were much smaller: only one per cent of pupils had taken anything in the previous week. Cannabis smoking accounted for nearly all of the illicit drug use among school pupils. The amount of heroin use was tiny: less than one per cent of the pupils had ever taken it.

Although the use of illicit drugs by any school pupils is rightly a matter of concern, the small numbers involved should reassure parents and teachers that Portsmouth and Havant do not have a drugs epidemic on their hands. Further, if we are realistic, the fact that hardly any of the drug abuse involved heroin must also be reassuring. We do not wish to play down the social and legal problems associated with teenage cannabis use, but it is important to recognise that the health hazards associated with cannabis use are on a par with alcohol and tobacco, and therefore the health problems involved with school pupils' drug use can be considered along with those caused by drinking and smoking. This perspective is made all the more appropriate by the fact that most of the drug users were regular drinkers and smokers.

Alcohol, tobacco and illicit drugs: relationships with other factors

The relationships between the use of any of the legal or illegal drugs and objective factors are surprisingly small. Age was the exception, with the older pupils smoking, drinking and taking illicit drugs more commonly than the younger pupils. Although there were differences between girls and boys, these were not systematic, and any suggestion that girls are less likely than boys to drink, smoke or use illicit drugs is not borne out by this survey. There seem also to be few relationships between parents' occupations and the consumption of drugs.

Some relationships are evident when it comes to leisure and life-style. Those who drank and those who had experience of illicit drugs were not expected home as early as others. Smokers, drinkers and those who had used drugs had more out-going leisure activities, visiting pubs and going to parties more often than others; those with experience of drugs also went to the cinema or theatre more often. Those without drug experience spent more time involved with family-centred leisure. None of these associations are surprising, but it might be expected that the smokers, drinkers and drug users would also have had more pocket money, or more earned money: in fact there was very little difference between them and the others in this respect.

The substantial differences between those using drugs and the others were those of attitude. There were small differences over the extent of agreement and disagreement with parents and expectations concerning job and exam prospects: drinkers, smokers and drug users had a marginally darker view than the others, but the relationships were slight. The real differences were over the the answers to the question on 'risks': drinkers and smokers were more likely than others to say they would do the things listed in the question, and the relationship was even stronger for those with experience of drugs.

What are we to make of this strong relationship between the 'risks' question and the consumption of legal and illegal drugs? Its meaning is far from straightforward, mainly because the items in the question represent several different types of risk and the combinations of responses could tap several different underlying psychological dispositions. It should also be remembered that the pupils' responses are not evidence of actual behaviour; the question was in effect an invitation to pupils to give an impression of the type of person they saw themselves to be.

The items contained in the question can be seen in Table 3.8 and in the sample questionnaire. They represent different types and levels of risk. Some of the activities are mildly unhealthy, some are physically dangerous, some are illegal, some are socially frowned on; most are in fact combinations of two or more of these things. For some of the items, the activity's acceptability and the extent of the risk is related to the pupil's age or sex: accepting lifts from strangers and missing a day of school are examples. The responses to the battery of items cannot be sensibly lumped together as a single variable called 'risk', because of these differences of meaning. By adding together the core risks then averaging them for different groups of pupils, as we have done so far, we have been condensing the data in a crude way.

We can speculate about what may lie at the psychological base of the pupils' responses. As a first step, we can identify five dimensions that these questions might be tapping. They are: a fondness for physical danger; a general wish to show courage or daring; a genuine lack of appreciation of risks; a rebellion against authority; and a longing for adulthood. A full analysis would probably come up with more underlying reasons for answering 'yes' to the risk questions, but the present example are enough to make two points. First, the five dimensions are not just aspects of a general 'risk-oriented' disposition: they represent five distinct candidates for explaining the 'yes' answers to the questions. Secondly, we cannot tell from our data which of them was really at the base of our drug-users' high scores. There are some indications that rebellion was more important than a fondness for danger (the lack of any relationship between drug use and the dangerous sports item, for example), but a proper investigation of this would require a much more extensive battery of questionnaire items and a thorough statistical analysis using multivariate tools such as factor analysis.

Whatever psychological factors lie at the root of the drug users' high scores on the risks question, the implications for health education in this field are clear. School pupils will not be put off tobacco, alcohol or illicit drugs by horror stories or by simple admonishment. If anything, an approach that emphasises danger and illegality will only encourage those already likely to be interested in smoking, drinking and taking drugs. The approach currently encouraged by the Health Education

Service in Hampshire acknowledges this point and treats drug education as part of general education for skills required in adolescence: skills for individuals to make rational choices. The results of this survey are a vindication of that approach.

Our final point about prevention and health education returns to the links between smoking, drinking and the use of illicit drugs. The survey results show that the illicit drug users came mainly from the ranks of the smokers and drinkers. Smoking is associated with illicit drug use more strongly than anything else in the survey: a quarter of the regular smokers in the survey had used an illicit drug. Whether or not smoking and drinking contribute in a causal way to the development of illicit drug use, it is clear that they are strongly related, and must be tackled together. It should also be remembered that among young teenagers, nearly all their drug-taking behaviour is illicit, whether it is confined to legally available drugs or extends to illegal drugs: cigarettes and alcohol are illegally purchased and consumed. The dealer in illicit drugs is one of our society's most potent symbols of wickedness and danger to young people; perhaps attention should also be turned on those otherwise respectable retailers and publicans who illegally supply young people with cigarettes and alcohol.

4 DISCUSSING DRUGS: INTERVIEWS WITH USERS

During 1986 and 1987 we carried out an interview survey of illicit drug users in Portsmouth and Havant. We interviewed 41 men and women with a wide range of drug histories and personal circumstances. The main aim of the survey was to provide a descriptive account of the lives of a substantial sample of local drug users and their attitudes towards different aspects of drug use. Other parts of the project have provided facts and figures that might seem impersonal and divorced from the human problems that are at the centre of public concern about illicit drugs. There are many myths and fears about drug users, and the recent media coverage of the issue has done little to help people come to a balanced understanding of the facts. This section of the report is intended to provide a window on the local drugs scene, in the hope of clarifying some of these matters. The survey was also designed to provide supplementary information on local levels of drug use, and some validation of our other findings on current trends among users and in the local market.

The survey sample was not intended to be representative of all drug users in the Portsmouth and Havant area. We wanted to concentrate on opiate use and, more specifically, on heroin use. In a representative sample of illicit drug users a majority of people would be users of cannabis alone, because the use of cannabis is relatively widespread, and opiates account for a only small section of the illicit drug market. We have concentrated on heroin partly because of the scale of public concern about it, and partly in recognition of the seriousness of the individual problems associated with it. We should also point out that our methods of contacting informants largely ruled out random sampling: there was an element of random selection in the choice of informants from the Northen Road Centre, but for the rest of the sample we tried to get interviews with all the users we could find. However, the interviewed users were a diverse group, as the paragraphs below will show. Nearly all of them had histories of opiate use but also had experience of several other illicit drugs.

The diversity of the users' experiences and characteristics is a theme that we are forced back to repeatedly when discussing this survey. Accounts of the lives of drug users have often tended to build up a picture of a typical user, but it turns out that this idea is unhelpful. Drug users differ greatly in their family background, personality, views on drugs, and personal history of drug abuse. There are some common threads, but it would be wrong to see in these interview results a composite picture of a 'typical drug user'. There is no such person.

The survey

Contacting the users

The aim was to interview a variety of drug users, including some who were not known to the Northern Road Centre. We used several methods to contact potential informants. To begin with, we mainly approached people known to the agencies working with drug users, but towards the end of the project most of the contacts were made through other drug users. First, we went to the probation service and the social services. We gained the co-operation of the local heads of these services and then spoke individually to social workers and probation officers. They then approached clients they knew to be drug users and asked if they would agree to be interviewed. If their clients agreed, we were put in contact with them.

Secondly, we went to the Northern Road Centre. We picked a random sample of drug users currently on the Centre's client list. A letter was sent from the Centre to each of the selected users explaining the nature of the research project, and giving assurances of anonymity and confidentiality. Initially users were asked to contact the Centre to say whether or not they would agree to be interviewed. Few replied to this letter, so we wrote to a new randomly selected sample of users, again through the Centre. We then called in person to talk to the users in more detail about the project. This produced a much better response.

Thirdly, we met some people at a drop-in group for drug users. Only one user was approached directly for an interview, but by attending the group we made ourselves known to several users who later agreed to be interviewed.

Fourthly, we traced the social networks of users through our initial contacts. Our original contacts asked other users if they would agree to be interviewed. If they did, then we made arrangements for the interviews, either through our original contacts or with the new users themselves. We did not meet any of these users until they had agreed to be interviewed. Making contact with users through third parties was extremely time-consuming. It involved repeated telephone calls and visits both to professional workers and to the users we already knew. Not only did we have to find the users through third parties, but we also had to make the detailed arrangements for the interviews in the same way: finding a place, date and time convenient both to researchers and to users took a lot of effort. There were also instances when appointments were not kept and the whole process of arranging an interview had to be started again.

Fifthly, we went with the users we already knew to places where other users met, to speak directly to them about the project and to ask if they would agree to an interview. This method proved a swift way to secure interviews. Because users could meet the researchers, they were better able to ask questions about the project and discuss any worries they had about the purpose of the research. We found that users' concerns about confidentiality were better dealt with face to face than through a third party. A few users we interviewed were extremely helpful in putting us in contact with others, both by asking users themselves and by taking us to meet them.

Our original aim was to interview between 40 and 75 users, and we had hoped that the total would be near the top of this range. However, we had more difficulty finding and making arrangements with informants than we had expected, and the 41 interviews we achieved took place over a longer period than originally planned. These difficulties were very frustrating at first, partly because our initial perception of the size of the local drugs scene was an overestimate. Later on, the information from the prevalence study put our experiences in perspective: the estimates from the prevalence study and the schools survey suggest that our sample is equivalent to some five per cent of all the regular opiate users in the area in any one month.

All but one of the informants lived within the Portsmouth and Havant local authority boundaries, and they were spread equally between the two.

The interviews

The interviews took place between October 1986 and August 1987. Each drug user was interviewed by one of the two PSI researchers. The length of the completed interviews ranged from about 45 minutes to two and a half hours, and the average time was about an hour. Users were able to ask specific questions about the research before and after the interview, and most often these were about confidentiality and the purpose of the project. Often we talked informally with the users for some time as well; many showed considerable interest in the project and wished to see the results when published.

All users except one agreed to the interview being recorded on tape. For practical reasons, one other complete interview and parts of two others were also recorded in writing. We used a check-list of questions in the interviews to obtain the information in a comparable form, but we allowed each interview to develop in areas of particular interest. We asked for background information such as age and employment status, then asked questions about drugs: parents' and siblings' use of drugs; informants' own drug use; how they started to use; how they perceived their use in positive and negative ways; their health; involvement with the police; contact with drugs agencies; their friends' drug use; stopping using drugs; their plans for the future; and what they thought of the Government's anti-heroin campaign.

Some older users said they thought that younger users would be more suspicious about research on drugs and would therefore be less likely to co-operate. They also admitted that if they had been approached themselves when they were younger, particularly when their drug use was not known to any of the authorities, they would have been wary about being interviewed. Several users said that their main concern had been about whether we wanted names and addresses of other users or dealers. One woman who was present when her husband was interviewed commented that she had previously refused to be interviewed because of this worry. Although older users had similar anxieties, they often balanced them against the fact that they were known to the authorities anyway. A user with a police record joked about this, saying that there was nothing we could tell the police that they did not know already.

The majority of informants were both articulate about their drugs careers and knowledgeable about drugs. Many of them had read a considerable amount about the physiological and psychological effects of drugs, and the more broad-based drugs literature. Once the initial hurdle of making contact and gaining confidence had been cleared, most users were happy to talk openly with us.

For the purposes of analysis we transferred information from the tapes to paper in a summarised form. We constructed a 'proxy questionnaire' based on the check-list of questions used in the interview. We were then able to fill in the responses from the taped interview. This put the information into a manageable form for analysis.

Background characteristics of the informants

Sex and age

Table 4.1 shows the basic characteristics of the users whom we interviewed. A quarter of them were women. This was a slightly higher proportion of women than among users registered at the drugs centre, where about one in five clients were women. It would appear from our own observation, and from the more recent referrals to the Northern Road Centre, that women now made up a higher proportion of drug users than they had done in the past, and this fits with evidence from research in other areas. This is important, because often the 'typical user' is assumed to be a young man.

Table 4.1 User interviews: background characteristics

Numbers of users

TOTAL	41
Female	11
Male	30
Age	
Up to 20	3
21 to 25	11
26 to 30	10
31 to 35	10
36 to 40	6
41 to 45	1
Domestic background	
Married/Cohabiting	
- with children	12
- without children	4
Lone parent	4
Single, living alone	9
Single, share flat/house	5
Live with parents etc	7
Housing tenure	
Council house or flat	14
Owner-occupied	10
Private tenant	9
Lodger/B & B/Hostel	4
Housing association	1
Tenure unknown	3
Employment status	
Employed full-time	13
Employed part-time	4
Looking after children, full-time	5
Unemployed	19
Other information on the unemployed:	
Some informal work	6
Looking for work	1
Voluntary work	1

The majority of users were aged between 21 and 35. Only three users interviewed were aged 20 or less, and only one was over forty years old. Most of the people in the study started using drugs in the middle of their teenage years, and this meant that their drug histories covered about ten years. Some of the older ones, however, had been using drugs for about twenty years. It is likely that our group of users contained a smaller proportion of teenagers than the drug-using population as a whole in Portsmouth and Havant. As we said earlier in the report, younger people were wary of meeting anyone considered to be a figure of authority, including researchers.

Housing and domestic background

The housing circumstances of the users were more varied than might have been expected. One third of the users lived in council houses or flats. A quarter lived in owner-occupied property, but several of them were not the owners of the property - they were living with their parents or other relatives. Another third of the users lived in privately rented property of some kind: nine as tenants, and four with shorter-term tenures, in lodgings, bed and breakfast accommodation or hostels (Table 4.1).

Over a third of the informants were living with a partner; some were married and others were co-habiting. Most of these couples had children. Four other users were lone parents. In total 16 of the 41 users had children and were living with them. Several others had children with previous partners and no longer lived with them.

One third of the users did not live with a partner or with their family, although a number of them had rooms in houses or flats shared with others and therefore could not strictly be said to live alone. Seven users lived with their parents or other older members of their family.

Employment status

Table 4.1 also gives figures on the employment status of users. Nearly half of users were unemployed and had no responsibility for child care, although six of them mentioned that they sometimes earned money by working 'on the side'. One did voluntary work, and another was actively seeking work. A few had been unemployed for many years and seemed unlikely to be working in the near future.

Seventeen of the users had paid jobs, although three of those jobs were funded under one or other of the government special schemes. In addition, five of the men and women we interviewed had primary reponsibility for child care within their family, an occupation which carries as much responsibility as a paid job.

Which drugs ?

The next few paragraphs are devoted to the actual drugs used by the survey informants, and to the use of drugs by members of their families and by their friends.

Table 4.2 summarises the information we collected about drugs they were taking when interviewed and drugs they had taken in the past. Current use is shown in two columns: for each drug, column (a) shows how many informants made any use of it, even if infrequently and in small amounts, and column (b) shows how many informants used it regularly. The other two columns show the same information summed over each users' whole drug history: column (c) gives the numbers of users who had ever used the drugs, and (d) gives the numbers who had at some time used them on a regular basis. It should be noted that columns (c) and (d) cover the whole of the users' lives, including the present. Because of multiple drug use and changes from one drug to another, it is possible for a user to appear more than once in a column, and each column therefore adds up to a total greater than the sample size.

Alcohol is included in the table, but it is considered in a different way from the other drugs. Alcohol is a legal drug and most adults drink it, so it would not be useful to include moderate social drinking in the same table as the use of illegal drugs. When alcohol is used for severe or regular intoxication, however, it is of interest as part of a pattern of drug abuse and we have therefore included it in the table. Use of alcohol is included only if users admitted they had bouts of drunkenness or a constant intake of alcohol. Occasional drunkenness is not included.

Table 4.2 User interviews: present and past drug use

Numbers of users

	(a) Any use now	(b) Regular use now	(c) Any use at any time	(d) Regular use at any time
Opiates				
Any opiate	31	24	40	38
Heroin	21	12	38	36
Methadone	16	14	28	22
Codeine linctus	3	1	15	3
Others (mostly Diconal)	8	5	28	18
Barbiturates	1	0	15	5
Tranquillisers	5	4	20	9
Cocaine	2	0	27	2
Amphetamine	8	4	39	28
Cannabis	26	10	39	21
LSD/'Magic mushrooms'	1	0	28	8
Solvents/Glue/Gas	1	1	5	2
Alcohol (see note below)	19	10	29	21
Nothing	3	3	-	-
TOTAL	41	41	41	41

Notes:

(1) Alcohol is only included in this table if it was part of the informant's problem drug use. See text for details.

(2) Note that users often took more than one drug, so all the columns add up to more than the total number of informants.

It is unlikely that the figures for the drugs used at any time (column (c) in the table) are entirely comprehensive. Sometimes, late in the interview, users would mention drugs that they had omitted in the earlier accounts of their drug histories. We must assume, therefore, that some users failed to mention some of the drugs that they had used.

Current use of drugs

It is difficult to summarise the drug habits of the people in the survey, because most of them used more than one illicit drug. They tended to use different drugs at different times, rather than taking them in combination. Two-thirds used opiates; over half used cannabis; and half were heavy users of alcohol. Smaller proportions used amphetamines (eight people) and tranquillisers (five people). Very few of the informants were using cocaine, barbiturates, hallucinogens or volatile inhalents (glue, solvents and gas). Three informants at the time of the interview were drug-free. Although we did not actually record tobacco use, it was difficult during the interviews to ignore the fact that most users also smoked cigarettes.

Although users did not stick to one drug exclusively, they tended to concentrate on one and to use it regularly, with casual use of other drugs in the background. Most of the informants who used opiates took them regularly; of the 31 who used opiates at all, only seven limited themselves to occasional use. About half of the regular opiate users took methadone on prescription, and nearly all the others bought heroin or Diconal on the local drugs market. One used codeine linctus, bought legally from chemists. The other people in the sample were very mixed: amphetamine, cannabis, tranquillisers and alcohol were each used regularly by a different group of three or four people, and one person used a volatile inhalant. None of the informants were regular users of cocaine, hallucinogens or barbiturates.

Some of the informants had a more serious drug habit than others. Among the opiate users the range was from occasional smokes of heroin when someone else was paying, through to prescribed daily methadone supplemented with black-market heroin and Diconal. Those classed as 'regular users' were using at least once a week, and a majority of them were daily users. Among those who did not use opiates, most were using amphetamine, cannabis, tranquillisers or alcohol on a daily basis, but some were heavier users than others. For nearly all of the people we interviewed, however, drug use had at some time been serious enough to cause a major disruption in their lives, as we shall see later.

The fact that over a third of the informants were in paid employment demonstrates that, for some users, behaviour was less impaired by drugs than for others. This is partly a function of the type and amount of drugs used. Light users of drugs found it relatively easy to live an otherwise normal life, and users of cannabis seemed to have few problems about work, even when their use was heavy, but users of opiates and heavy users of amphetamines had more difficulty. Among opiate users, the ability to hold down a job did not seem to be related in a simple way to the frequency and level of dosage. Some of the working addicts were on daily methadone and, although the daily use of heroin was more of a problem for employment, some of the regular heroin users also had jobs. Methadone is generally a stabilising influence on drug users, because it takes away the perpetual necessity to find illicit heroin and to get money for it. It keeps users 'straight', meaning that it takes away the uncomfortable feelings that physical addiction brings on whenever the last dose wears off, without badly incapacitating users (methadone has little euphoric effect), and it can get them off the hectic roundabout of 'scoring' drugs illegally. There can be little doubt that one factor behind unemployment among daily heroin users is the life-style necessitated by the use of an expensive and highly illegal drug, which makes them very busy but very unreliable, with little time for anything other than drugs.

Drug histories

The currently used drugs tell only a small part of the story. We have already drawn attention to the fact that many of the informants had long histories of drug use. Only one person had used one drug exclusively throughout: a young man who inhaled butane gas. Some of the others had at one time or another taken a very long list of different drugs. We hesitate to say that any of them had sampled the full range of illicit drugs because it is almost impossible to make a comprehensive list of all the substances that are swallowed, smoked, inhaled and injected by drug users - there are many different psychotropic substances, and most come in several different forms.

In this report we constantly refer to a core list of three illicit drugs, or, more accurately, three groups of drugs: cannabis preparations (herbal cannabis, cannabis resin, and the concentrated extract tetrahydrocannabinol, known as THC), amphetamines (such as dexedrine tablets and amphetamine sulphate powder), and opiates (such as heroin, morphine, methadone, Diconal and codeine linctus). All but three of the informants had used drugs from all three groups. This does not mean that most of the users had had periods of sustained use of all the core drugs, but it does mean that they had some experience of all of them. This can be seen in columns (c) and (d) in Table 4.2. Nearly all the informants had tried opiates and had become regular users at some time, but there was a group of people who had taken amphetamine and had not become regular users of the drug. And although most informants had smoked cannabis, only half had at any point had a period of heavy, regular use.

Cocaine had been used at some time by two-thirds of the informants, but only two of them had taken it regularly; the contrast between these figures illustrates the fact that cocaine is a drug that our users have sampled (some on several occasions) but has not become a significant part of the local drugs scene. Two-thirds of the informants had taken hallucinogens such as LSD and 'magic mushrooms' and more of them had used them regularly than in the case of cocaine: eight of the twenty-eight had gone on to regular use.

Twenty of the informants had abused benzodiazepine tranquillisers, and fifteen had abused barbiturates; there was some overlap between them - nine of the barbiturate group were also in the tranquilliser group. Nine informants have had a period of regular use of tranquillisers and five had had a period of regular barbiturate use; two of these were the same people, so in total thirteen of the informants - one third of the sample - had had a period of regular use of sedative drugs of either type. Only five of the informants had used glue, solvents or gas as drugs, and only two of them had had a period of sustained use.

Many informants had experienced alcohol problems at one time or another. Accounts of drinking behaviour were not easy to obtain because users had a tendency to underestimate the seriousness of their alcohol consumption, perhaps because drinking is legal and they were not pursued and prosecuted for it. Drink had been used excessively by over half of the informants. From our own experiences with them, we know that many still supplemented their other drug habits by drinking, sometimes in heavy bouts.

Cannabis was still used by two-thirds of our informants, and many had been casual cannabis users throughout their drug histories. Many did not regard it as an important element of their personal drug use, and often treated it as a normal part of the culture in which they lived, in the same way that most people see drinking alcohol as part of the wider culture in this country. When we asked about the drugs taken at any point in their history, users would typically finish with '...Oh yes, and a bit of blow' ('blow' is a slang word for cannabis). A small number particularly enjoyed cannabis and paid more attention to it, but in general our sample of users did not represent the large majority of illict drug users in Portsmouth and Havant, who restrict their use to cannabis smoking. Two of our informants were using cannabis alone, but they had used other drugs in the past.

Compared with the generally long term use of cannabis, the use of amphetamines and opiates tends to be in patterns of stop and go. Individual histories are often made up a string of discrete episodes, each defined by its emphasis on a particular drug. These phases of drug use can be many and varied. This is illustrated by one man, now in his mid-twenties, who started drinking heavily and using cannabis when he was 14, then became quite seriously involved with amphetamines at the age of 18, then stopped using amphetamines and started using heroin when he was 20. Another user illustrates how numerous the different phases can be: between the ages of 12 and 35 he went through separate phases of using alcohol, cannabis, amphetamines, heroin, methadone, amphetamines with alcohol, methadone, methadone together with heroin and amphetamines, and finally methadone on its own again. Often such multi-stage drug careers are peppered with periods of abstinence of varying length.

These examples also illustrate something which is of fundamental importance when trying to understand users with multi-drug histories: although the effects of amphetamines and of opiates are quite the opposite of each other, there are times when users will happily switch between them. There are two reasons for this. One is that users sometimes become dissatisfied with the drug they are taking, because they no longer enjoy its effects, dislike its side-effects or cannot afford it. They deliberately change to the other drug. The other reason is that users' motivation for drug-taking is sometimes just to shift themselves as far as they can from normality, using whatever is available, and they go over to another drug in the face of a change of circumstances related to drug supply or to their surroundings. Several users told us that what they were seeking at some periods of their drug-taking was 'to get out of their heads' in any way they could, rather than to enjoy a sensation of a particular type.

Over time, the choice-based changes seemed to predominate. In the early stages of their drug careers, users might have switched because they were unable to obtain the drug they previously used, but later on a more discerning approach was evident, as users built up knowledge of the effects of different drugs and an understanding of their own reactions to them. We think this was behind the general trend in many of the users' drug histories away from amphetamines and towards opiates. Such a change was apparent in about half of the informants' drug careers. We could dismissively explain the move by saying that opiates are more addictive than amphetamines, and are therefore bound to get the upper hand eventually, but often the process seemed to involve a conscious rejection of amphetamines. Several users looked back on their periods of amphetamine use with loathing.

Having said this, we should point out that users differ in the apparent control they exert over the direction of their drug-taking. Some seemed to have more control than others; some had even given up recently or reduced their drug-taking to a minimum. Others had a more chaotic pattern, with much switching and multi-drug use. We need to be careful in interpreting these apparent differences of control, because they do not necessarily indicate fundamental differences between individual personalities. We already know that users tend to go through various periods of heavy use, light use and abstinence during their drug careers, and a snap-shot survey of a sample of users is bound to find some people with a serious habit and others in a relatively calm phase. We also have to be careful about users' own statements about the degree of control they exercise over their drug taking. Some were keen to give the impression that they had everything under control, and were critical of users who did not; our view is that some of these statements reflect anxiety about addiction and could be wishful thinking. A few users had a completely different attitude - they looked down on some others who in their eyes were not 'real junkies'. Even this could be interpreted as bravado in the face of the unpalatable reality of their own addiction.

How did it start?

All of the users started with illicit drugs while they were teenagers. Half had tried their first illicit drug before they were 16 years old. Six of them first used when they were 13, a further nine when they were 14. All but three had started before their 18th birthday.

For three-quarters of the informants, cannabis was their first illicit drug. Thirty-two started with cannabis, although two of these used other drugs as well right from the start: heroin in one case and tranquillisers in the other. Three users started just with tranquillisers. The remaining six users all started with different drugs: LSD, cough linctus, heroin, cocaine, butane gas, amphetamines with LSD, and amphetamines with barbiturates. Some users, however, started their problem drug taking prior to this, with alcohol. Most of the informants had experience of alcohol before illicit drugs (the schools survey shows that most young teenagers try alcohol, so this has to be regarded as normal), but at least six users had regularly been involved in bouts of heavy drinking.

We asked users why they first started to take illicit drugs, and whether it was a choice they made or just something they fell into. Two-thirds said they had deliberately chosen to use, but for a number of different reasons. The most common reason given was curiosity: about drugs that their friends were taking or about drugs that they had read about or seen on television. Six users indicated they were much taken with the spirit of the times, and wanted to become part of the alternative culture which embraced drugs ('I was a bit of a hippy'). Some users, however, said they had chosen drugs because 'it was the cool thing to do', or felt that it put them above the crowd.

Eleven users said they had not really chosen to use drugs. They said they had just come across them and it seemed natural to take them.

Some had been passed their first joint at a party or at a friend's house, and they had accepted it without thinking too much about it.

Most of the users took their first drugs with friends or relatives. Over half of the informants specifically mentioned their friends or relatives when we asked about the circumstances of their first use of an illicit drug, and most of the others implied it (for example, 'I just came into contact with it at school'). Only four said they had got their first drug from a dealer, and two of these said they had gone to the dealer on their own initiative. The way one user started was plain bad luck: he was filling his lighter before going to bed, in a hostel, when a room-mate pointed out how to use the fuel as an intoxicant.

Few knew much about illicit drugs before they started taking them. This is interesting in the light of the 'choice' that most of them said they made. However, four were so keen that they had read up on the subject of drugs before they tried any. Some mentioned that they had known about the risks of addiction, but others had not. One user said 'All I knew was that other people took them and didn't die.' One said the risk was the thing that made it all so exciting.

Most of the users moved at some point to heroin, or to another opiate, but generally this was after a number of years taking other drugs. Only eight started opiates before they were 18, but three-quarters of opiate users started on them by the time they were 22. Several commented that it was only after a long period of use that they became dependent; a few took opiates for some time and were still able to give up when circumstances demanded it.

The reasons why informants' drug use moved away from the use of cannabis alone were very varied, and no general pattern emerged. Some graduated to harder drugs because the people they mixed with were taking them. Some threw themselves into multi-drug use with enthusiasm because they 'didn't like normality' and liked the personality changes that drugs bring about. Some experimented with heroin just once and liked it so much they continued to take it, although others said that their first experiment with heroin was a horrible experience, and they had to persevere to acquire the liking for it. Some started to use amphetamines heavily to give them confidence in social situations. One person moved away from cannabis-only use when she was unable to obtain any and a dealer offered amphetamine tablets as a substitute. One young woman moved on to heroin because she was intrigued by the media publicity.

When we asked whether they could have avoided drug use, half said no. The others speculated that they could have avoided drugs, some saying that things would have been all right if they had not come into contact with drugs at all. Two users thought that if there had not been so much conflict with their parents, then they might have not used drugs. One said, 'It sounds corny, but it was my little rebellion'. He came from a family background with a combination of violence and religious fervour. Some users gave reasons why they thought their drug use could not have been avoided. Four said that taking drugs was something they had really wanted to do. One woman said that she had been curious about drugs since she was very young. Three felt that they had been destined to become drug users.

Family use of alcohol and illicit drugs

We asked users about their knowledge of drug use by their parents (or guardians) and by brothers and sisters (Table 4.3). As with their own use, we classified alcohol differently from other drugs: we recorded any incidence of illicit drug use or prolonged use of prescribed psychoactive drugs, but recorded alcohol use only if it amounted to a problem. The figures refer to use either in the past or at the time of the interview.

Nearly a third of the users said that one or both of their parents had abused drugs or alcohol. Ten of the users' fathers had abused alcohol and one had used illicit drugs. Four of the users' mothers had used prescribed psychoactive drugs, and one had used illicit drugs.

The majority grew up aware of their parent's abuse. Only one user said that his parent's use was subsequent to his own. Others spoke about incidents associated with their parents' use of drugs or alcohol, remembered from their childhood and youth, and although they may not have fully understood their parents' use at the time, they were certainly conscious of it. A few told us vivid stories about their father being drunk or about taking their mother's pills.

Table 4.3 User interviews: family abuse of drugs

Father	
Alcohol	10
Prescribed drugs	1
Illicit drugs	2
TOTAL	11
Mother	
Alcohol	1
Prescribed drugs	4
Illicit drugs	0
TOTAL	5
Brother or sister	
Alcohol	4
Prescribed drugs	0
Illicit drugs	11
TOTAL	15

A substantial number had brothers or sisters who had been users: over a third in all, mainly of illicit drugs rather than alcohol. A few of the users had brothers or sisters who had histories of heavy drug use that were similar to their own, but, for the most part, informants did not have the same patterns of consumption as other members of their families: they differed in terms of when they started, what types of drugs were used, and how heavy their use had been.

Friends

The social life of most of the users we interviewed was built around others who used drugs. Twenty-seven said that most of their friends used drugs. Two said around half their friends were users; nine said they knew a few other users. One was a lone user, and always had been. One had given up his social contacts with the drugs scene, to try to come off. One informant refused to say how many of her friends also used drugs.

Most said that their friends used a whole range of drugs, including opiates, but two specifically said that although they knew other users, none took opiates. Some were at pains to point out that other users should be counted as acquaintances, not friends, because drugs were the only things they had in common, or because their friends were unreliable, even disloyal. Because the drug scene is built on a foundation of illegality and dubious commercial practices, it is inevitable that an air of mistrust pervades relationships. We should however make it clear that among the drug users we also observed many close relationships, a lot of mutual support, and above all a feeling of subversive comradeship.

Dealing

Twenty-five of the informants had sold drugs to others at some time. Ten of them had been involved in dealing in large amounts, mostly of heroin and amphetamines. Most were not dealing at the time of the interview.

These surprisingly large numbers illustrate the point that the distribution network for drugs does not comprise a small number of non-using pushers touring the area selling to addicts and novices. Among the users of drugs other than cannabis, people are often drawn into the business of supplying others, most of whom they know. Most sell drugs because their own habit is expensive and because it is difficult to sustain a full-time job while putting in the hours that are necessary in order to maintain supplies. Of course people do sometimes attempt to increase sales by attracting new people to drugs, or to the particular drug they are selling, but the 'luring' can also operate in the opposite direction: users can lure others into dealing. This is illustrated by the story of one of our informants : once she had sold a small amount of a drug, she was driven more and more into dealing by acquaintances who pestered her to obtain further supplies.

Trying to understand

In the interviews the drug users said many things that helped us towards an understanding of their behaviour. Some of the more important points that emerged may help advance understanding of the factors behind drug abuse and how to reduce it.

Men and women across the country want a simple answer to a simple question: why do drug-takers do it? People who have no contact with illicit drug use see it, understandably, as an irrational activity, one that has a high personal cost in terms of health, money, legal trouble and general squalor. They feel that there must be an explanation. What tips people over the edge into a habit that to others seems unthinkably self-destructive? Surely there must be something that distinguishes the potential drug user from the rest of us, some characteristic or experience, some psychological disposition or physical trait. And if we could find the explanation, then surely something could be done about it. Unfortunately, a closer look reveals that the issues are not so simple. The question 'why?' certainly has no single answer, and it may be an unhelpful question. To explain what we mean here we need to consider the more familiar example of two legal drugs, tobacco and alcohol, both of which are associated with health risks and other problems. Illicit drug use is far outside the experience of most people and our argument is more easily understood if we ask the same question about legal drugs: why do people drink, and why do people smoke?

An attempt at an answer would include a mixture of social, psychological and physiological factors. The social factors brought into the analysis would be complex: there are the pressures to drink and smoke in order to conform or to mix socially and, distinct from these, the valued effects of tobacco and alcohol to help ease tensions in social situations. In addition, there is the problem of where to draw the line between socially generated motivations and pure pleasure-seeking. This cannot be found in the comparison between the lone drinker and the party-goer, because it is not obvious why someone reaches for a drink when alone - is it because of a lust for the physical effect, force of habit, a physical dependence or a learned response to emotional pressure? Nor are the party-goers' motives more easily interpreted - they could be drinking as participants in a happy social ritual, or simply using the opportunity to indulge in their favourite drug on an occasion when it is more acceptable to drink to excess. The psychological and physiological factors are just as confusing, because the boundary between physical addiction and psychological dependence is disputed. When smokers and problem drinkers return to their habit despite the known health hazards and social problems, are they responding to a physical urge or a desire for emotional comfort, or both? If the a is both, then what are the relative strengths of the two elements?

Even if we come to grips with the problems of understanding continued abuse, the matter is made even more complex by the separate question of why people do it in the first place. Are people who start smoking different from those who do not? And how does moderate social drinking become problem drinking? The factors that initiate these habits are unlikely to be the same as those involved with their persistence. We would not expect the reasons for a teenager's party excesses to explain a seasoned drinker's nightly sessions.

We could go further into the ramifications of the simple-looking question 'why do they do it?', but this analysis is enough to show that the question quickly develops into a mass of more complex issues. The same is true for illicit drugs, and much of the analysis is the same as for alcohol and tobacco: the question splits up into problems of weighing up social, psychological and physical factors, separating the logic of starting drug abuse from that of persisting, and so on. It should be clear, therefore, that the information collected in the survey cannot provide a simple explanation for drug abuse. What we can do is record the users' own experiences and their views on drugs, and do it in a way that will contribute to the wider debate about drugs and drugs policy. In particular, we hope that this account can help people to leave behind some of the myths and prejudices about drug misuse.

User's views of positive and negative aspects of drugs

Every informant was asked what he or she liked and disliked about taking drugs. We tried to explore all of each user's views on the positive and negative aspects of drugs by following this up with a less personal question, enquiring what were the good and bad aspects of drugs. The users expressed a wide range of views, both personal and general, and nearly all had something to say on both sides. Likes and dislikes varied between individuals and between drugs, and people pointed out that changes occured over time: for example, some users who once enjoyed the feelings brought on by amphetamines now found them unpleasant.

Most informants were quick to say that they liked the physical feeling and the immediate psychological impact of drugs. These comments

ut all types of illicit drug. In relation to heroin, users
eling of security that it induced, shutting out worries,
int of oblivion. They said that it was relaxing and
that the sense of well-being could be compared to being
nket. A few also said that it perked them up and helped
h things - a surprising comment, given the generally soporific effect of the drug. More predictably, other users said they liked (or used to like) the feeling of alertness and energy that came from taking amphetamine. Cannabis was mentioned less often than other drugs, probably because users did not rate it as an important element of their drug intake; people mainly referred to its effects in terms of sociability.

As well as these points about specific drugs, positive comments were made on the physical and psychological effects of illicit drugs in general. Some liked drugs because they stopped them feeling normal, and one went as far as saying 'Even if I have something that makes me not feel very well, sometimes I'd rather have that than feel totally normal.' Others said they particularly enjoyed 'the rush' when injecting drugs: intravenous administration results in a very fast passage of the drug to the brain, and a sudden onset of the drug's effects. Although this was mentioned in regard to injecting generally, it came up most often in reference to the specific use of Diconal.

Other positive comments were related to emotional and social factors, and to the personality changes that can be brought about by drugs; three users even claimed that their mental health had improved as a result of illicit drug use and another said that without drugs he would have killed himself. Many said that heroin made their awareness of problems fade away. There was clearly a tendency for users to turn to heroin or other opiates when they suffered emotional shocks or crises: several recounted incidents when they responded to disruptions of family relationships by shutting out the problems with opiates. Others said that at some time they had used amphetamine to boost their confidence or shed inhibitions in social situations: this was largely their reason for using amphetamine when they were teenagers, faced with the trials of socialising at parties, discos, pubs and clubs. Two users told us that they would be happy for drugs to take the place of their social relations with other people: one man said that he could imagine life consisting of sitting next to a pile of the stuff and doing nothing else, and a woman that she could imagine life without companionship as long as she could have amphetamines. Another informant described opiates as being 'everything you need'. For some users, however, the social side of drug abuse was part of the pleasure. They said that they liked the drugs scene and their hectic life within it: one heroin user said 'The sad fact is I love it all'. Some users specifically valued the identity that participating in the world of illicit drugs had given them.

On the negative side, users said that they disliked a number of general things about drugs: addiction, the sordid side of the drugs scene and the people involved, and the unpleasant personality changes that they had experienced. Most of the comments were not related to specific drugs, but amphetamine was singled out for criticism by several users because of the personality problems it caused. The problems of addiction and withdrawal were mentioned by half the users in this part of the interview, and others mentioned it when talking about other subjects.

At various points during the interview, the users mentioned the health problems they had all experienced as a result of taking illicit drugs (these are discussed later). Some users also spoke about mental health problems, although it was difficult to interpret these comments because they overlapped with other comments about personality changes and addiction: there was considerable variation in the extent to which different users regarded their drug habits as medical, psychological or social problems.

Many of the problems of drug abuse stem from its illegality and from the way the illicit drug market operates. Five users specifically said that illegality itself put them off drugs; others said they disliked the trouble that it brought them, both from the police and from the general problems of obtaining supplies on the black market. Others pointed out that some of the worst health hazards result from the illegal status of drugs: they said that needle-sharing and the adulteration of drugs with dangerous 'cuts' would not happen if the drugs were legally available. A lot of users also complained about the price of illicit drugs.

Users made critical comments about the social consequences of taking drugs. Whilst some said they liked the drugs scene, others said they hated it, and disliked the people involved, whose only shared interest was drugs. Some users said that they were unhappy with the person they had become, and that drugs had made them selfish and dishonest. Drugs had caused trouble with other family members and seriously strained relationships, some beyond breaking point. However, it was impossible to judge whether drug abuse alone caused couples to break up, because there were always other problems involved, and we were not in a position to weigh up their relative seriousness.

When discussing what they liked about opiates, and heroin in particular, users often mentioned its ability to buffer their problems and cut out the the rest of world. Some, however, pointed out that the real result was the opposite of what was intended: when ignored, problems did not go away, but tended to get worse. And on top of the original problems others piled up as a result of the legal, health and social repercussions of drug misuse. When people did manage to stop using, they found that their problems had multiplied.

Specific drugs for specific problems?

It should be remembered that many of the users' comments concerned specific drugs, rather than drugs in general, and that most of the users had concentrated on different drugs at different times over the years. This suggests that at least some of them switched deliberately from one drug to another to get a different effect. What lay behind these changes? One explanation could be that what drug users have in common is trying to meet social demands by resorting to chemical intoxicants. As those social demands change during a person's life, so the appropriate drug changes.

To illustrate this, let us consider one pattern that we mentioned earlier, a pattern that occurred in almost a third of the informants' drug histories. These users began illicit drugs with cannabis, then took up amphetamine, then moved to heroin or other opiates. It can be argued that there is a logic to the pattern in terms of the social demands on young people as they grow up through their teens and face the world as a young adult. Cannabis is a drug that alters the mood, and users feel that it enhances sociability: it is not hard to understand why teenagers enjoy it as they encounter new social situations that they find awkward and testing. Amphetamine is a drug that bolsters confidence in social settings, and makes outgoing behaviour easier. Young people who have real difficulties mixing can be drawn to it. In this respect, amphetamine is a tougher drug than cannabis: the changes of mood and personality that it produces are more intense, and several of the people we interviewed admitted that they had used it to sweep away their shyness and inability to communicate. Having established a pattern of drug abuse to tackle social demands, it is not surprising that some people turn to opiates when more substantive problems arise: if you perceive yourself to be the problem, you might use cannabis and amphetamine to change yourself, but if the problem is external, and you see it as being out of your control, you are more likely to turn to a drug that shuts it out. Thus drug abuse starts as a way of enhancing social relations, or even as a tailoring of the personality, but becomes a method of social retreat.

Stopping

Some insights into the informants' reasons for continuing drug use are to be found in their comments about giving it up. Most of them were about social and emotional difficulties, rather than the physical problems of withdrawal. This may not be an accurate picture of the short-term problems, because most heavy opiate users were fearful of the discomfort of withdrawal, but they did not see this initial hurdle as the real barrier to becoming drug free. Whilst it is not new to point out that dependence is much more than physical addiction, it is important to note that users themselves were aware of this, and recognised that in the long term other things bind them to drugs. Some might even fall back on a fatalistic version of the argument as an excuse to postpone attempts at withdrawal: why should I go through all the pain if there are other factors that will drive me back to drugs anyway?

Most users had at some time wanted to stop taking drugs. The reasons they gave were fear for their health and fear of sliding uncontrollably into a drug-oriented life. Some also said that trouble with the police or financial troubles had led them to want to give up. Four of the users, however, said that they had never wanted to stop, at least not permanently.

Many had had periods of abstinence from drugs, including breaks in their use of opiates. These periods had in some cases been long, up to five years. Although some were enforced - in prison, for example - most had been voluntary. Many of the informants stopped after a phase of drug use that seemed to be getting out of hand, but for some the conditions for abstinence seem to have been a period of stability in their lives, particularly regarding family circumstances. For them, the arrival of children or the establishing of a home seemed to have been a trigger. There were negative aspects of drugs that pushed people away from them, but there were also positive events that pulled people away from drugs.

Most users said that they had tried to stop taking drugs. A few of them had been successful, either in giving up altogether or reducing from multi-drug use to cannabis use alone, but many more had failed. Others had stopped using one drug only to replace it with another. Those who had stopped usually took more than one attempt to achieve a drug-free state.

We asked people why their attempts to give up drugs had gone wrong. Some said they had simply slipped back. Some mentioned that they had not replaced drugs with anything else in their lives. One woman said that without drugs she was a nonentity. She also said she could not handle deep emotions and could never remember being happy except when using drugs. But many attempts to come off drugs seemed to have foundered when another crisis came along: a relationship going wrong, for example, or a death in the family. In some cases old problems had not gone away, and it was just a matter of time before drugs became an escape again. Even those who had become drug-free still had problems in their lives and could still be at risk: people with heavy drug habits become detached from conventional life and the broken ties mend slowly. And if a return to drugs seems to offer a way to relieve the anguish, there is a risk that the clock will be turned back.

The vast majority of users said that they planned to stop using drugs, and some envisaged particular conditions which would enable them to do so, such as settling down to family life. Some planned to give up certain drugs but not others. For example, a few said they would continue to use cannabis but cut down on hard drugs. Other users did not plan to stop altogether: some heroin users in particular wanted to make it an occasional event only. One man said that he intended to reduce his habit to 'dabbling' with heroin; previously he had tried to give up drugs, but found the idea of total abstinence too difficult to cope with. Another user said he aimed at 'control' of his use: not to give up permanently, but to have periods of abstinence from drugs. He did add that amphetamine was a damaging drug and was 'going to have to go'. A few users said they doubted they would give up. One methadone user said 'Never...I've given up deluding myself.' Although most wanted to give up, many users were worried about whether they would succeed in the long term. One woman, who had recently limited herself to only very occasional use (although her alcohol consumption had increased over the same period), said she did not want to go back to drugs, although to say this seemed to her to tempt fate. She explained that she had often vowed to stay off drugs: 'Seriously, I don't want to go back to them...You get scared of saying you're not going to take them, because I've said that so many times...' Another user saw herself as on a 'wheel' of drug use. As she stopped using one drug, she replaced it with another. Her history was one of illicit drugs, then sleeping tablets, then anti-depressants and then alcohol; her own interpretation of the problem was that she had an 'addictive personality'.

The majority of users said that they knew people who had given up drugs (although it should be noted that the users invariably assumed that 'giving up' meant giving up opiates and amphetamines, and did not mean abstaining from smoking cannabis or abusing alcohol). Only eight said they had not known a single person give up. We asked them whether they remained friends with the people who had given up drugs, and nearly all said yes. This is quite important: it demonstrates that some people are able to give up hard drugs without cutting themselves off from their user friends for ever. There is more evidence for this in the histories of the users themselves: with two exceptions, the people in our sample who had given up hard drugs (or massively cut down their habit) were still in touch with other users. They may have broadened their circle of friends, but they had not deliberately shunned their old ones.

It is true that staying off drugs is very difficult while remaining in the same group of friends and acquaintances, whose lives (and conversations) often revolve around drugs and who often look down on ex-users and non-users as people who cannot keep up with them. But it is not impossible, and for some people it may even be important that they remain in contact with the drugs scene, in order to learn ways of saying no without feeling they have lost face. Some people probably have to remove themselves from the social pressures to use drugs; others can learn to cope with and resist those pressures, and if they can do this, so much the better. Saying no to drugs by avoiding other users is fine, but a chance encounter can renew the temptation.

The future

Most of the users made constructive and optimistic comments about their future life. Most hoped to have a future free of drugs or with occasional use only, and no-one admitted wanting a future of heavy drug use. These long-term hopes contrasted with the short-term expectations discussed above.

In many ways the plans of our informants were quite traditional. They revolved around work, the home and family life. Nearly half mentioned wanting to do something associated with work - many mentioned getting a job or a better one. A number said that they wanted to settle down and have children. Users' plans also frequently included home improvements or moving house, even buying a place. Some others mentioned travelling abroad. Only three users said they had no plans for the future at all. Two other users were unsure about their immediate future because of pending court cases.

Some said they were cautious about taking things too quickly, and were keen to maintain some stability in their lives. They were worried that too many changes could create a feeling of uncertainty and thereby lead to an escalation of their drug use. Others found it difficult to talk about the future because of the disorder of the past. One user said he wanted to do something constructive with his life, but could not see this happening. He said that his talents had always been modest, but they had been further impaired by drug use, and he 'can't think straight'. The most he could do was 'drift along'.

We asked about how users saw drugs in their future. Nearly a third said not at all, although different users talked of different time-scales. Younger people seemed more confident about giving up - perhaps because of their shorter drug careers. Several users said they did not expect ever to give up cannabis use. Some of the users on methadone prescriptions expected them to remain a feature of their lives for the forseeable future and in most cases this was because of the stability that the drug had brought to their lives. One of the methadone users who wanted to continue his prescription said that as long as the drug was a stabilising influence the issue of withdrawal was not important, because the drug was neither shortening his life nor doing anyone else any harm. But many of those using methadone were also worried about the process of withdrawal and seemed frightened at the prospect of life without it. One case illustrates a dilemma faced by some methadone users: a woman said that if she had a job and was occupied, then she might be able to come off methadone without returning to black-market drugs. However, she felt that she would not be able to cope with methadone withdrawal at the same time as a job. If, on the other hand, she tried to withdraw from methadone while she was unoccupied, she would be likely to start on illicit drugs again.

Problems

There are many indications that people who abuse drugs do it in an attempt to deal with social demands, and often simply to escape from problems. Is there any evidence that the users in our survey had had more than an average share of problems in their lives? The question cannot be answered with confidence, for obvious reasons: one cannot measure and compare the varied problems that different people experience, and anyway we have no group of matched individuals for comparison. Some of the users we spoke to had led unremarkable lives except for their drug taking. Our subjective assessment, however, is that a disproportionate number of our informants had suffered setbacks and tragedies in their lives. Some ran away from home and some were told to leave; others were involved with crime unconnected with drugs, especially theft and motoring offences; several were expelled from school; others had stormy family relationships, as a child or as an adult, or both; others had experienced difficulties forming personal relationships.

This is not to say that their problems had led directly to their drug abuse, but to point out that their lives were fertile soil in which a problem-oriented drug habit could germinate and grow. Responding to social and emotional demands with drug abuse sets up a cycle. There is more trouble with the law, more family conflict, more disruption of employment, and less money. People heavily involved in drug abuse become criminalised and poor, and find themselves with little stake in civil life: they become outsiders. The importance of their former identity is eroded, and therefore they have less and less to lose. So it becomes impossible to distinguish between the problems that might be at the root of their drug use and the problems that flow from it.

We explained earlier that a third of the users we interviewed had parents who had misused alcohol, prescribed drugs or illicit drugs, and several others had drug users among their brothers and sisters. It can therefore be argued that members of their families have set them an example: the way to deal with problems was to reach for a drug of some kind for support or intoxication. If their experiences as teenage drug users seemed to prove that drugs helped to meet social demands, then the family's lesson was reinforced, and drugs became the way they confronted adult problems. While their early drug experiences may have helped them enter into social situations, making their adolescence less anxious and more fun, their more recent drug use was to escape from problems, reflecting more closely the example of other family members.

Health problems

We asked users whether drug use had adversely affected their health. All but two users said that it had. The details need to be treated with caution, because we have not verified that drug-taking was in fact responsible for the ailments mentioned, and it is likely that drugs were sometimes blamed for illnesses simply because they were the other prominent 'medical' feature of users' lives. One user, for example, blamed his bronchitis on heroin, despite the fact that he smoked cigarettes. On the other hand, some users failed to attribute health problems to their use of drugs despite some fairly strong evidence to that effect: for example, both of the users who denied having drug-related health problems had had hepatitis.

The most commonly mentioned problems were those relating to weight loss and to intravenous administration of drugs, although others told us about a number of other specific problems with their teeth, digestion, chest, kidneys, and even eyesight. A few users just said they were more lethargic as a result of their drug use or said they were not as fit as they should be.

Thirteen users had at some time suffered loss of appetite for long enough to lose a substantial amount of weight, although none of them were seriously underweight at the time of interview. Both heroin and amphetamine have a tendency to reduce the appetite, but most of the informants were eating regularly and reasonably (this is discussed below). Five users also said they had experienced stomach or intestinal problems, including two who mentioned constipation; given the fact that heroin is renowned for slowing the digestive system, one might have expected these figures to be higher.

Many of the users mentioned problems associated with the intravenous administration of drugs. We can be fairly confident about this information since these complaints do have a direct relationship with injection. Eight users had had hepatitis (although we do not know whether this was type A or B). Eight users said they had problems with their veins or circulation: six of them said they have had abcesses, and others mentioned problems such as 'bad fixes' (caused by dirt or impurities entering the bloodstream along with the drug), phlebitis (inflammation of the walls of veins), or bad circulation.

Seven users claimed that their teeth were bad as a result of drug taking - a relatively large number for a single complaint. Some attributed this to the use of amphetamines, others to the use of oral methadone.

Seven users claimed improvements to their physical health as a result of their drug use, although most of these need to be looked at with scepticism. Two were pleased to have got thinner, having been overweight before, but the others had dubious ideas about the effects of drugs. Two users said that drugs had stopped them catching colds, and one man said his bronchitis had stopped as a result of using drugs. (These effects are more apparent than actual, because heroin use suppresses the cough reaction and generally eases the misery of cold symptoms; another user specifically mentioned to us that heroin users did not notice colds.) Two thought that drug-taking was linked to longevity and rejuvenation: in support of this, one said that she thought she looked young for her age and sometimes felt very young, and the other said that a lot of long-term users he knew looked young for their age. Our own observations did not support these views.

Diet

The majority of users had had periods of their lives when their diet was poor. Some users may have had an unbalanced diet for years at a time. They tended to eat only sweets or snacks during periods of heavy drug use, and some users hardly ate at all. At the time of the interview, however, the majority of users seemed to have relatively good diets. If users had one square meal a day, as well as lighter meals, we classified them as having good diets.

A minority of informants said that they kept up good diets even when using heavily. For some of them, force of circumstances meant that they had meals: some lived or worked where a meal or meals were provided; some users lived with their parents; one user ate large meals when at work, since his job was physically demanding; others had to provide food for their children, and themselves maintained a reasonable diet because of this. Other users, however, forced themselves to eat. They were conscious of the health problems caused by a poor diet and ate meals despite a lack of appetite. One man said when he was using heavily he drank Complan (a drink with a balance of nutrients), ate fresh fruit and took vitamin tablets. Another said he made sure he visited friends whom he knew would give him decent meals to supplement his diet of microwaved 'TV dinners'.

Needles

One of the main public health concerns about drugs is the sharing of hypodermic syringes among users. Needle sharing enables the transfer of disease because infected blood from one user is passed into the bloodstream of another. In the past the spread of hepatitis has attracted most attention, but currently there is concern about the spread of the virus which can lead to Acquired Immune Deficiency Syndrome (AIDS), and during the course of our research preventive policy was under debate locally. This included provision of health education literature and the introduction of a needle exchange scheme.

We asked users specifically about their use of needles now and in the past. The results are shown in Table 4.4. Nearly all informants had used needles at some time - 38 out of 41. Nearly all of these needle users had shared needles. Only two claimed never to have shared. At the time of the interview, just over a third of informants used needles, and about a third of this group said they still shared.

Table 4.4 User interviews: use of needles

Use needles now	14
Used needles in past	38
Share needles now	5
Shared needles in past	36

We found a high awareness of the risks of sharing needles and of the transmission of AIDS amongst users. Some users were very worried about AIDS and indicated that this was the reason they no longer shared needles. However, there was a tendency for users to claim initially that they would not share and later admit that in some circumstances they would. When we questioned them more closely, some said that if faced with the choice of sharing a needle or having to go without a fix, they would probably share. One user even said that in the past he had shared with someone who told him she had had hepatitis, and speculated he might do the same thing with someone who had AIDS. The users emphasised that good intentions evaporate in the urgency of the moment, and several were sceptical about the potential success of needle exchange schemes for the same reason.

Many of the informants used drugs less often than they had in the past, and some used needles only occasionally. Given their awareness of the risks associated with sharing and the circumstances in which they used drugs, it may be they were better able to plan for needle use and to ensure they had their own needles at the time. They might also have chosen to administer drugs in other ways if they had no usable syringe of their own.

Problems with the law

All but three of the users had been arrested in the past, and several were currently in trouble with the police. Thirty had been arrested for drug offences. Most of the drug offences were simple possession, but some were possession with intent to supply. Two others had avoided arrest for actual drugs offences but had been caught for thefts from chemists and GP surgeries. Six others had avoided arrest for drugs offences but had been picked up for other crimes, involving theft or violence.

A large proportion of users had criminal records simply because of the illegality of drugs or because the cost of drugs led them to raise money illegally. Many users had records of several types of offence, but 13 had been arrested for drugs offences alone (excluding motoring offences). Most of the other offences were carried out to get drugs or raise money for drugs: a total of six chemist or GP break-ins, 18 cases of theft or receiving stolen goods, and five cases of fraud, mostly with stolen cheques and credit cards. Ten had been arrested for violence of some sort, and one for carrying a weapon, but only one of the cases of violence was in any way related to drugs or drug use. That was a case involving amphetamine and alcohol used in combination. We found no evidence to connect heroin use with acts of violence.

As a result of their convictions, the users received sentences as follows (these figures refer to each user's most serious sentence): 13 users had spent time in prison and one had been to a remand home; a further ten had spent time on probation; three had been sent instead for psychiatric care or to Alpha House; the other 11 had received suspended sentences, fines or cautions.

We asked whether the trouble with the law had initiated any kind of help with their drug problem; most users said no. When they appeared in court, some users were referred to Alpha House (2), Highclere (1) or a psychiatric hospital (1). One user was given therapy when in prison. Two said they had been referred to the Northern Road Centre by the police after their arrest, but none of the others said they had been given any advice by the police or the prison service. One claimed that the only advice he received in prison was from a doctor who was astonishingly callous: the user asked for help with his drug problem, but the doctor had said that he should kill himself by cutting his wrists, and advised on the most efficient way to do it.

We know that some users had been guided towards help by their probation officers. Apart from personal counselling by probation officers and encouragement to attend the Northern Road Centre, probationers were offered the benefit of informal discussion sessions for drug users held at probation centres, where they could talk about their drug problems and meet drug advice workers.

Some users were very bitter about the police, and felt that the enforcement of the drug laws was a game played at their expense. A number expressed the view that the arrest figures were more important to the police than the drugs problem itself. In support of this argument they cited the publicly-stated police attitude of concentrating on heroin and on dealers, and said that this was contradicted by the disproportionate number of users who were arrested for possession of small amounts of cannabis.

Drug supplies were available to most users when they were in prison, but some said the drugs were expensive and they were unable to use anything except cannabis. Some had taken the opportunity to come off drugs altogether, but started again when they were out. A matter of concern must be the sharing of needles, which was much more common in prison than was outside. One user said that by coincidence other inmates had hidden a syringe in his cell before he had arrived and they later asked him to retrieve it for them.

The government's campaign against heroin

In 1985 the Government launched a campaign to dissuade young people from using heroin. There were advertisements in the press, on radio and television, and on hoardings in the streets. On the whole, the users we interviewed were sceptical about the benefits of the campaign, but a few thought that it might have prevented some people using heroin. Some suggested practical improvements, but many thought that the basic idea was wrong because any advertising glamourises heroin use. Many also thought the campaign was inaccurate in its portrayal of heroin users.

There were three main critical responses to the question, and each was mentioned by about ten users. One group thought that the publicity might put the idea of heroin use into some people's minds or make heroin appear exciting. One user said 'any publicity is good publicity'. Another thought it amounted to an advertisement for heroin, and he was particularly concerned about its effect on children. Another user based his opinion on his own experience when he was young: after watching a television programme about cannabis he decided he wanted to try it, and subsequently did so. The case of one young user seemed to prove the point about the anti-heroin campaign: she said that the recent publicity about heroin had made her interested in trying the drug. It made her wonder why so many people got into it, and she decided to try it for herself. At that time she only knew one person who had used heroin. She spent three days seeking out the drug, and was eventually able to buy some. Despite her own experience, she said that the television advertisements might put people off heroin.

The second group of users said that they thought the campaign had no effect. Some also said that nothing could stop someone determined to try heroin. One young user said 'it's a load of rubbish...people make their own minds up'. Three people said it would certainly not have any effect on anyone already using heroin.

The third group said that the campaign was inaccurate and too alarming. One informant said that 'scaring people rigid' was ineffective. Once people realised that the portrayal of heroin users was too extreme, then they would stop believing any of the health education information about it. Another user said that using scare tactics underestimated people's common sense, and he thought that most drug users were aware of the risks of heroin anyway. There were, however, a few users who argued that the campaign was not explicit enough, and felt that the shock and scare tactics should be pursued further.

Help from drug agencies

A number of the users in the sample had been drawn from among the clients of the Northern Road Centre. The others were contacted through the social services and probation service or via other drug user contacts, and we did not expect to find a large proportion of them to be touch with Northern Road. In total, 19 were currently in touch with the Centre, although more were officially 'on the books' there. By 'in touch' we meant in regular contact, even if that contact was an infrequent interview, as in the case of some people on stable maintenance prescriptions.

There were, however, another 14 users who at some time in the past had been to the Centre, to the Highclere detoxification unit, or to the clinic that was held at St James' Hospital before the Northern Road Centre opened. More than three-quarters of the users had therefore been in touch with Portsmouth's main drug advice services at least once. Three others had instead been to a clinic or rehabilitation centre outside the area. In total, five of our informants had spent time at Alpha House, the rehabilitation centre at Droxford. Only five users had never been to any clinic or centre.

Fourteen of the informants were using drugs prescribed by the Centre. Six others had been prescribed drugs from the Centre in the past but were now free of hard drugs or were buying them on the black market. Thirteen informants had spent time in Highclere.

Those who had at some time been to the Northern Road Centre gave us their views about the service. Most of their comments fell into four general subject areas: comments on the running of the Centre, and on the Centre's staff; comments on the subject of methadone prescription; comments on the running of the detoxification unit; and comments on the general issue of help with coming off drugs.

Comments on the running of the Centre

Many of the users made favourable statements about the Centre, its policies and its staff, but these were often tempered by complaints of a very practical nature. Our general impression was that users valued the Centre as an open facility; several were explicit about this, saying that it was a comfort to know that there was always someone they could turn to. The staff had clearly built up close relationships with some users, who talked of them with warmth and respect. As we said earlier in the report, we think that the proportion of local drug users who were prepared to contact Northern Road was increasing. The Centre was certainly not seen as a hostile institution, and was not identified with drug law enforcement, despite its links with the probation service; none of the users we spoke to questioned its assurances of confidentiality.

The practical complaints related to a number of aspects of the Centre's work, varying from the hours when staff were available to the accuracy of the equipment for urine testing. One practical point mentioned by at least six users concerned the way in which people were dealt with after initially contacting the Centre. New cases were usually discussed at a special meeting held each Wednesday, where doctors, community psychiatric nurses and other staff members worked out what sort of help to offer them. Sometimes the users themselves attended the meeting. This way of dealing with new cases was both open and sensitive, and we heard no complaints about it in principle. A problem arose when a user found the commitment (or plucked up the courage) to approach the Centre for the first time and went there on a Thursday or a Friday, and then had to wait nearly a week to find out what the response would be. The users we interviewed said that a week was a long time in that situation, and it was a severe test of someone's resolve to seek treatment. We should make it clear that people were not turned away and told to come back next week: they were seen by a member of staff who took down their details and discussed their drug problem. Most of the anxiety came from the users wanting to know whether or not they would get a prescription for methadone.

A small number of users made unfavourable general comments on the Centre and its staff, along the lines that they were kind and meant well but were naive and amateurish, or did not really understand the way that drug users look at the world. Only one user was thoroughly disapproving; she did not say why she felt that way.

Comments on methadone prescription

These were particularly numerous. Most of the users curently in touch with Northern Road were taking prescribed methadone and nearly half of the previous clients had been on methadone at some time. They had mixed views about its benefits as a substitute for heroin. Out of the twenty with experience of prescribed methadone, six made unfavourable comments about it. They said that it was harder to come off than heroin itself, was less pleasurable, and was merely a way of 'keeping straight'. In a way methadone fits the popular image of an addict's drug better than heroin itself: people take methadone because they need it to get through the day and because they fear the pain of withdrawal, and not because they get any particular 'high'.

An identical number made favourable comments about it, however. They said that it had helped stabilise their lives, which had become chaotic as a result of the constant roundabout of finding money to buy heroin, then buying it and taking it, then finding more money, and so on. One user said that an emotional crisis unconnected with drugs led him to increase his heroin intake massively and in desperation he contacted Northern Road where he was put on methadone; he later came off it, but he was convinced that it saved his life on that occasion. Other stories were less dramatic, but the common elements were a removal of the disruption caused by illicit opiate use and a chance to devote time in their daily lives to something other than drugs. Some people we spoke to were on long-term maintenance prescriptions, and had been able to rebuild their lives around their families and their work. But even those favourably disposed to methadone treatment said that it was harder to give up than heroin. Four of the users thought that treatment centres should return to a policy of prescribing heroin.

A lot of the users made comments to the effect that addicts tried to exploit the availability of methadone from Northern Road: they approached the Centre without any aim of coming off, but with the intention of supplementing their drug supply. We also found evidence that some methadone was sold on to other users, but this made up a very small part of the local drug market. Methadone may not be most addicts' first choice, but it is an opiate and it is a good reserve drug if heroin is unavailable. A minority of users really liked it, mainly because its effects are longer lasting than those of heroin. The problem of users exploiting the policy of prescribing heroin substitutes is not a new one, and has always dogged the work of drug clinics. Drug workers have to show some trust in the people who have come to them, ostensibly for help, and cannot work on the assumption that everything users say and do is suspect.

Some of the methadone prescription was for long-term maintenance, but for many users the aim of the Northern Road Centre was to reduce the dosage gradually, eventually to zero. This often seemed to happen after a period of stable dosage, when they were ready to cope with a phased withdrawal. The users we spoke to were nervous about this reduction. One said that they were worried that once they embarked on it, there was no going back to the old level of dosage if the attempt failed. There was something in this: it would be a foolish withdrawal programme that left it open to users to request and receive an increased dosage as soon as they had problems, and there was therefore some pressure on people to stick with their reduced prescriptions. However, the Northern Road Centre made decisions about clients on an individual basis, and the guidelines about prescriptions were applied flexibly. Perhaps the concern felt by users about the 'point of no return' in the reduction of their prescription was a part of their general anxiety about giving up something which has become very important to them. Several users also said they were worried about changes in treatment policy at national or local level, in case their supplies of methadone were reduced or stopped altogether.

Some users argued that the Centre was mean with its assessment of the correct dosages of methadone. In part, this was only natural: people want more of what they like, and some will always say they do not have enough. But some were also confused by the fact that prescriptions were assessed individually, and if they saw their friends with larger dosages than their own, they thought had been cheated. Inevitably, the involvement of different staff at different times, and the real difficulties of assessing an appropriate dosage, meant that there really were some inconsistent decisions, and this compounded the problem.

Those prescribed methadone were expected to give up their use of black-market opiates. Several users said that as a consequence users just told lies about their other drug use, for fear of having their methadone prescription cut. Since the whole basis of their attending the Northern Road Centre was open discussion of their drug use in order to get help, this was an absurd state of affairs. But it was also a difficult one to resolve. When an individual is in the early stages of a programme based on substituting methadone for heroin, the Centre does not need to insist that he or she abstained from other opiates, but later, as a substitution programme develops, the switch away from street drugs is its very essence, and the Centre is right to insist on it.

Comments about the Highclere detoxification unit

There was a built-in bias in our survey when it came to comments on Highclere. Since most of the people we interviewed were current users, there were hardly any 'success stories' about becoming drug-free. Only one of the thirteen people in the sample who had spent time in Highclere was currently drug-free. It is important that this should not be taken as a measure of how effective or ineffective the unit was, because it is merely a feature of the way we selected our sample: we sought out people who were still taking drugs. As a result, most of their comments on Highclere were negative ones.

Several users said that they went into Highclere because they had an impending court case and needed to demonstrate that they were doing something to give up drugs. Others thought that most people went into Highclere for that reason, and not to try genuinely to give up. But others went there in good faith: we met users who had gone in order to become drug-free.

There were comments to the effect that within the unit a hierarchy had developed, based on patients' previous drug habits: the patients who had the more serious habits became socially dominant. This may have been connected to the fact that some people went there with no real intention of giving up, and one would not expect this atmosphere to be conducive to a rejection of drugs. Some said the big problem in Highclere was that there was nothing to do except talk about drugs with the other patients. Added to that, there were organised discussions among patients, and these focussed on drugs, as part of the therapy. Users said that withdrawing from drugs in a place where people hardly ever talked about anything else was hard work.

General comments on help with coming off drugs

Some users made points about drug withdrawal and rehabilitation that were not specific to the local services. One point was that coming off drugs was easy when compared with staying off, and services should therefore be aimed at long term help with the rebuilding of people's lives as well as help with withdrawal. Another point was that the services should trust users more (although this contrasted with the claim that users often failed to tell the truth about the drugs they were using).

Others pointed out that because some of the work of treatment centres and other facilities for drug users involved group discussions, they inadvertently assisted the illicit drug market by bringing together people with an interest in drugs. Several users told us that at one time or another they had valued such meetings because through them they found new contacts and new sources of supply. This is another quandary for drug advice workers: to prevent the misuse of such meetings they would have to stop them altogether, but there can be little doubt that exchanges of experiences and views help users who are genuinely trying to give up. A related issue is the involvement of ex-addicts as drug advice workers: one user expressed disapproval of this, but another suggested that there should be more of them involved, because they understood the users' feelings better than people who had never had the same problems.

5 DRUGS IN PORTSMOUTH AND HAVANT

The aim of this study has been to open three windows on the problems of illicit drug use: the first by gathering together information on the drugs used, the numbers of people involved, and the characteristics of the local drug market; the second by going into the local schools and asking pupils about alcohol, drugs and tobacco as part of a survey about their leisure and their lifestyle; and the third by interviewing a group of local drug users about their life now and in the past, and about their views on drugs.

Diverse demands for better information

Different people want different things from this type of research, and we have had to be careful to consider local drug problems from a number of perspectives. People who work in the local drug services are looking for pointers to ways of improving prevention and treatment policies, and for help in planning for the future. They also need to know how far their work has penetrated into the local drug-user population, and whether there are particular ways in which it could reach more users. Other workers in the caring professions need to know the extent to which their client groups are involved in the world of drugs, and what particular drug-related problems they face. The police are keen to know the overall scale and nature of the local drugs trade, in order to compare it with the part that they already know about. Teachers and others in the education service are anxious to know whether illicit drugs are a real threat to their pupils, and want information to help them respond with the right preventive measures. Parents and other members of the general public want an analysis of the facts to set beside the confusing and alarming media reports about the escalation of drug abuse and its connection with the spread of AIDS. Some of the drug users also have their own hopes about the study: they want it to go some way towards putting their side of the story.

Unfortunately, there are no absolute answers when it comes to research on illicit drugs. It is a world of secrets, where people have to keep the truth from others and sometimes have to delude themselves. We have been lucky, because we have had unequalled access to confidential records from different agencies, and because many drug users spoke with us more freely than with people in positions of authority. But it is still difficult to piece together the true picture, and the issues at the root of drug abuse are complex and elusive. In this report there are findings which will be of use to all of the groups and individuals listed above, but in the end we have increased the number of clues rather than solved any mysteries.

Numbers

Everyone wants to know about numbers: how many illicit drug users are there? The question makes an assumption of uniformity among drug users, and it is not a valid assumption. Drug-taking is not an all-or-nothing activity: the population cannot be divided into normal people and junkies. There are many different illicit drugs, and they have very different effects, both in terms of their psychotropic qualities and in terms of the emotional and social impact they have on people's lives. Most drug users take only one of these drugs on a regular basis, and perhaps one or two others occasionally. Some people are only casual users of their particular drug, taking it at the weekend or whenever someone else gives it to them, while others are heavy, regular users, who let their whole lives revolve around the drug. Some people take different drugs in different periods of their life, and often leave drug-free gaps between these phases. Others, however, use only one illicit drug throughout. The question of how many users is therefore not a straightforward one.

The conceptual difficulties of asking 'how many users?' can be illustrated by analogy. If, for example, we ask how many local people are involved in politics, we run into a similar set of problems. First of all there is the issue of what we mean by 'politics': the activities of political parties would certainly be included, as would participation in local parliamentary and council election campaigns, but after that it is hard to know where to draw the line. Community groups, residents associations, trades unions, business associations and professional groups could all be included in the political arena, as could many people who are public employees. Then of course some of the people who fall under the umbrella of these organisations are keen and active whilst others are paper members only. Furthermore, in a given year some people will arrive on the scene while others will drop out. Thus it can be seen that the idea of a simple head-count of local people involved in politics is not a simple idea at all. It is also true for drugs; the numbers may be different, but the conceptual problems are the same.

It is easy to understand what is meant by an estimate of the number of under-fives in Portsmouth and Havant, or people of pensionable age, or manual workers, or registered unemployed. But there is no single definition of a 'drug user' that is at the same time useful and unambiguous. We are dealing with a wide variety of people, with drug use ranging from occasional cannabis smoking through to heroin addiction demanding more than one injection a day. A definition based on illegality is not the answer: it would leave out a person who began by drinking bottles of codeine linctus and moved eventually to a daily methadone prescription, with intermittent use of amyl nitrite, hallucinogenic mushrooms, solvents, tranquillisers, and injected alcohol. Someone could have a drug history like this without ever breaking the law.

In the final analysis, most people are concerned to know about the numbers of people involved with opiates and cocaine, and our research does throw light on these. The prevalence study also gives some idea of the scale of use of other drugs, but in much broader terms.

An overview of the drugs scene in Portsmouth and Havant

The illicit drugs scene is not a single thing, but a set of interlocking markets and groups of people whose social contacts are defined partly or wholly by their involvement with illicit drugs. Its largest part comprises the thousands of people who use only cannabis, whose actual number we can only guess at. In his definitive reference book 'Street Drugs', Andrew Tyler states that the estimated UK figure for regular users is about 2.5 million, and points out that even if the true figure is only half that, then the situation is one of mass law-breaking, with the consumption of about 600 tonnes of cannabis per year. If we stick with Tyler and halve the first estimate to just over one million users, and if the figures for Portsmouth and Havant are in line with the national average, then there are over 7,000 regular cannabis users in the area. Our view is that this figure should be taken as a minimum. In addition, there are others who smoke it occasionally.

Amphetamine comes second to cannabis in popularity, but again we can only guess the actual numbers using it. It is more popular with teenagers and people in their early twenties than it is with older drug users. Although there are probably thousands of users, it tends to be taken less regularly than cannabis: habitual amphetamine use has damaging psychological and physical effects that the regular cannabis user does not have to contend with.

The number of opiate users is much smaller. We have made a tentative estimate that in a single month there are in the region of 550 regular users of heroin, methadone, Diconal and other opiates in Portsmouth and Havant. The figures for notified users suggest that the local opiate problem is on a par with the rest of the country, and no larger than that; they also suggest that it is more stable than in the rest of the country, because the numbers of new addicts notified every year (and the numbers of former addicts who disappear from the records) are relatively low. The local opiate problem is smaller than in London and in Merseyside, because studies in those cities have shown a far greater annual number of opiate-related incidents and referrals per head of the population than in Portsmouth and Havant. Most of the illicit heroin comes from London, but some other opiates are of local origin:

prescribed Diconal tablets are illegally sold, and a small amount of prescribed methadone also reaches the black market.

There is a small and relatively stable market in LSD. It is mainly taken by people who are already users of other drugs; it has few regular users. Many drug users have also used hallucinogenic mushrooms, picked locally. The market for LSD is smaller than it was during the late 1960s and early 1970s. Cocaine is available on the local market, but it is a minority taste and is expensive; as in the case of LSD, it tends to be used only by people already taking other illicit drugs. We came across very little evidence of regular cocaine use, although a majority of opiate users have tried it at some time. We found no evidence of 'crack' in the area.

Our discussions with people in the caring professions and with voluntary workers suggest that in some neighbourhoods there is some solvent abuse, but we found little direct evidence of a substantial solvent problem. We were told that it is subject to changing fashions among young people. Solvent abuse has played little part in the drug histories of most of the people we interviewed, and it is not part of the local 'drug culture'.

A danger to society?

Illicit drugs are hazardous, but to whom? Is public anxiety really about the damage that drug users inflict on themselves, or is about the danger to the rest of us? There is a lot of confusion, and some dishonesty, over this point: sometimes people's own fears are dressed up as concern for the victims of illicit drugs.

Some of those fears are about violence committed by drug users. The image of the violent junkie is a persistent fictional device, and tales of drug-crazed killers abound, from the coke-heads of today's 'Miami Vice' back to the famed 'hashishiyyun' assassins of 11th century Persia (who, despite the myth, probably did not commit their murders under the influence of cannabis). More prosaic than this are the accounts of junkies mugging people for the price of their next fix on the streets of US cities. People are worried that the growth of illicit drug use is an element of a general decline into urban lawlessness, of dangerous streets and violent crime.

These fears are largely unfounded. In our study we came across very little evidence of violent crime associated with drug abuse. On the streets of Portsmouth and Havant, there is far more to fear from people who have been drinking than from drug users. One reason is that heroin and other opiates have the effect of slowing people down, making them dozy and contented - 'mellow' was a word we heard from several users - and it does not incline them towards violence. Cannabis, while not having the knock-out characteristics of opiates, tends to induce a contemplative, dreamy state, and users often behave in a slow and reflective manner; again, there is no tendency towards violence. When we began our fieldwork among local drug users, we had the same prejudices as everyone else, and we were apprehensive about the kinds of people we were going to meet. It should be remembered that we were interviewing people with a history of hard drugs, not casual users of cannabis. In the event, the users we met were civil and helpful, and they often made us feel welcome. Some were naturally suspicious of our motives at first, but they were never threatening. We cannot say that they were just like any other group of local people, because most of them had led lives that were out of the ordinary, but we can say that their behaviour never made us doubt our own safety. Many of them were pleasant company, and this made the interviews enjoyable for us.

Although opiates and cannabis do not push users to personal violence, there seems to be some truth in the reputation of amphetamine as a drug that produces erratic and sometimes violent behaviour. The only case of apparently drug-induced violence that we came across among our informants concerned amphetamine used in conjunction with alcohol. The same is likely to be true for cocaine: one user was stabbed in the face several years ago during an argument with someone who was 'high' on cocaine. In both of these cases, the person concerned may have been disposed to violent behaviour in the first place, and the drug may have played only a small part in precipitating the incident; nevertheless, the effects of stimulants such as amphetamine and cocaine should be regarded with the same caution that one would reserve for alcohol - for some users, stimulants can enhance violent behaviour.

Although the public have little to fear from violence by drug users, there is a genuine problem of theft and fraud carried out to raise money for heroin and, to a smaller extent, other drugs. At the risk of labouring the point, we should say that it is a financial threat, and not a physical threat: we knew of no cases of street theft that amount to 'mugging'. Many of the people we interviewed had at some time been involved with shoplifting, burglary or cheque and credit card frauds; many of them had been prosecuted. At one time or another, a substantial proportion of heroin addicts resorted to this sort of crime to raise funds; at other times they managed to limit their consumption to a level they could afford from their legitimate income, or they supplemented their income by dealing in drugs themselves. Some regular heroin users steered clear of stealing and fraud altogether. Most cannabis and amphetamine users spent only moderate sums of money on drugs (often in line with a daily drinker's alcohol bill), so they had no financial problems resulting from drugs, and therefore had no particular incentive to get involved with property crimes; the same was true for casual users of heroin.

A threat to our children?

One area of genuine concern among the public is the extent to which illicit drugs are a threat to children and teenagers. The survey that we carried out in the local schools shows that very few young people had taken illicit drugs. Below the age of 14, the number was negligible. Among the older pupils, 99 per cent had never tried heroin, and over 90 per cent had never tried any illegal drug. Although few pupils had tried illicit drugs, even fewer were regular users. Overall, only one per cent of all the 11 to 19-year-olds in the survey said they had taken anything in the previous week, and even among those aged 16 and over the figure was only three per cent. Most of the drug use reported by teenagers was cannabis smoking.

A much larger proportion of pupils in the survey said that they knew other people who had used drugs: a quarter of all aged 11 and over, and more than half of those past their sixteenth birthday. Many were therefore exposed in some way to the availability of drugs, but most of them did not take it up. In our own fieldwork in the community, we came across hardly any drug users aged under 20.

A worryingly large proportion of the pupils drank alcohol and went to pubs. Two-thirds of the older pupils, and one in five of the 11-year-olds, had had a drink in the previous week. Tobacco use was widespread too - a quarter of the older pupils smoked cigarettes. Few of the pupils who had tried illicit drugs had not tried alcohol and cigarettes first. The link between legal drugs and illegal drugs was strong, and was best illustrated by the fact that one third of all the regular smokers in the survey had tried an illicit drug.

Two-thirds of the users we interviewed said that they had started taking illicit drugs by choice, and the others seemed to have bumbled into it. Hardly any were given their first drug by a dealer; most started their drug use with relatives or friends. Reasons were difficult to fathom, but most seemed to have been curious about the effects of drugs or keen to demonstrate their rebellion against conventional life. This fits with the results of the survey of school pupils, which showed that the pupils who had experimented with drugs presented themselves as bold and rebellious, and were more socially adventurous than others.

Whether it was curiosity, rebellion or just a search for pleasure that prompted them at the start, a substantial number of those who kept on taking drugs did so for different reasons: many of those we interviewed indicated that they had used drugs to meet social demands, taking stimulants to build up their social confidence or taking opiates to switch off their problems. There was also evidence that a substantial group of the long-term drug users had witnessed alcohol or tranquilliser abuse by their parents, and may have learned at home that intoxication was one way of dealing with life's difficulties. Given that in the schools survey the drug users came from among the smokers and drinkers, this possible link between parents' behaviour towards legal drugs and their children's drug histories is quite important. If parents are worried that their children might take up drugs, then the simplest preventive measure might be to avoid drinking and smoking themselves.

Legal drugs

It is important that we consider, for a moment, the consumption of legal drugs. This was not the subject of our study, but many of the people we spoke to in the caring services said that they wished it had been. Alcohol, tobacco and tranquillisers cause addiction and damage to the local population on a far greater scale than illicit drugs.

Everyone knows about the dangers of tobacco addiction: the risks of cancer, bronchitis and foetal damage during pregnancy are well advertised, and nobody can reach for a smoke without picking up a packet bearing a health warning. Less well appreciated are the health risks of prolonged or immoderate drinking, or drinking during pregnancy; there is little publicity about alcohol hazards, with the exception of campaigns against drink driving. Tranquillisers are prescribed to many people, and many become addicted. Nobody knows how many tranquilliser addicts there are, but the figure could exceed half a million in the UK, dwarfing the problem of heroin addiction. Many people were referred to the Northern Road Centre because of a dependence on tranquillisers, and in the first six months of 1986 they equalled the number referred there because of illegal drugs.

The psychological, emotional and social consequences of the misuse of alcohol are far-reaching. Violence in the street and in the home, danger on the roads, neglect of children, damaged relationships, and ruined family finances, all these are hazards for the alcohol addict and for those near to him or her. Many users of illicit drugs think the hatred and fear that people reserve for their drugs is hypocrisy, given that society smiles on a legal drug that causes such widespread misery. People are shocked by media pictures of pale, broken-veined junkies, but can walk past equally derelict drunks in the park. They may not like the presence of the down-and-outs, and they may feel sorry for them, but people do not see them as drug addicts.

Bringing the argument closer to home, most people relax with a drink from time to time, and there is no harm in that, but few of them would see alcohol as using a mind-altering drug of similar potency to cannabis, although that is what it is. Many smokers are addicted to tobacco, probably because of the stimulant nicotine, another psychoactive drug. Many people rely on the caffeine in coffee and tea to brighten them up during the day. As we have said, many also rely daily on the calming effect of prescribed benzodiazepine tranquillisers. In our society it is quite normal to use chemicals to change the way we feel and think, and drugs form a part of many of our social rituals. Illegal drugs form only a tiny part of this all-pervading drug culture. There are special problems associated with the use of illegal drugs, but when looking at these problems we should place them against the background of almost universal legal drug-taking.

Problems for the users

So far we have considered the problems that illicit drugs cause for the majority of the population. What about the difficulties faced by the users, other than the fact of addiction itself? They can be put crudely into five categories: health, money, law, relationships and personal development. We have been at pains to stress that there is no typical drug user, and the same goes for their problems, for everyone copes differently with the trials of illegal drug use. A few manage to avoid arrest, keep on top of the costs of their habit, stay fairly fit and maintain a stable home life, while others are in trouble on all counts; most regular opiate and poly-drug users fall in between these two extremes. As far as the majority of illicit drug users are concerned, that is to say the people who use only cannabis, we have no evidence to suggest that they face any particular drug-related problems, other than the risk of trouble with the law.

Staying with the opiate and poly-drug users, we can list a number of health problems that arise: the direct hazards of overdosing and poisoning; general nutritional problems as a result of a loss of interest in food; and the many problems associated with intravenous administration. The illicit use of syringes leads to damage to veins, the passage of dangerous physical and chemical impurities into the bloodstream, and the spread of infection. Needle-sharing amounts to disease-sharing, and this is of particular importance in respect of hepatitis and the HIV viruses.

Money problems need little explanation. Buying a casual bag of heroin or amphetamine at the weekend is unlikely to be a financial drain on people with a regular income, but when it builds up to daily use, the cost is substantial. Unless a user's earnings are high, extra money needs to be found, so people start by selling their possessions, but often turn to crime, dealing drugs or getting involved with stealing of one kind or another.

Problems with the law are almost inevitable for heavy drug users. Possession of drugs is an offence, but possession of class A drugs, including most opiates and cocaine, attracts particularly high penalties. Dealing in drugs is regarded as an offence of the utmost seriousness, and a substantial proportion of users sell drugs at one time or another. Added to the fact that some users turn to other crimes to support their habit, these circumstances mean that sooner or later anyone with a serious drug habit will be arrested and prosecuted. It should be remembered that most legal proceedings under the drug laws are for cannabis possession, so it is not only users of hard drugs who risk prosecution.

A heavy drug user's relationships with his or her partner, other family members and friends can be affected in a number of ways. The health, financial and legal problems described earlier are all capable of causing major disruptions to family and social life: we do not need to spell out how illness, lack of money and imprisonment can damage relationships. But there are also less tangible ways in which problems develop between people as a result of involvement with illicit drugs. Trust between partners, or between parents and children, can dissolve as users resort to deceptions, half-truths and lies to cope with the disapproval of others. Family and friends may reject the user outright; in some cases this happens as soon as they learn about the drugs, but in other cases they try to help and understand the user but eventually give him or her up as a lost cause. Users can become emotionally changed by their addiction, and if they use drugs as a way of fleeing from responsibility and from life's problems, then they inevitably become unreliable and exasperating as partners, relatives or friends. Some users manage to keep their family relationships on a sound footing, but most go through difficult phases, and many suffer traumatic break-ups. For some, disentangling the family quarrels and other emotional difficulties from the use of drugs is a chicken and egg problem: it is quite possible that difficulties with relationships came first, and that drug abuse was a refuge from them. Even in these cases, it is very likely that drug-taking made the problem worse rather than better.

Perhaps the most intransigent problems faced by heavy drug users are in the area described by the term 'personal development'. Irrespective of whether their drug use is a matter of choice or compulsion, it involves them in a style of life that severely limits other options. Partly because of the time and money required to keep up a regular drug habit, partly because of the compound problems discussed earlier, and partly because of the relative social insularity of the hard drugs scene, users can find themselves with few choices for the future: many have plans and hopes for improvements in their employment and housing circumstances, but their life-style puts many obstacles in the way of these goals.

Some may not want to see their lives go along the tramlines of conventional family life and nine-to-five employment, but the fact is that their options for any alternative life-style, for travel and for independence, are limited by the demands and problems of their drug habit. Drug abuse seems to be one way in which people's lives can get stuck, bogged down in a mire of problems with their wheels spinning. Seeing the way out is not a simple matter. Among the people we interviewed, several have abandoned or radically changed their drug habits and as a result they have got moving, changing their life in constructive ways. For a few others, however, it has been the other way round: they seem to have reduced their use of drugs in the wake of a change in personal circumstances - a stable relationship or the arrival of children, for example.

Local services

We should make it clear that this research project was not designed as an evaluation of the local services and their effectiveness. Suggestions for those services do flow from our results, but mainly as a consequence of the general findings about the drugs scene and the lives of drug users. In the survey of individual users we did ask for their views about the Northern Road Centre, and those comments were reported in the previous chapter, but no part of the study was aimed at a direct assessment of any agency's work with drug users.

It is important to distinguish between the various objectives of the agencies working in the drugs field. Prevention is different from treatment; law enforcement is different from after-care for offenders; helping users with their day-to-day problems is not the same as helping users to give up drugs; and bringing people off drugs is not the same as keeping them off. A comprehensive local drugs strategy should take into account all the objectives of all the agencies (paying special attention to areas where there are conflicting objectives) and it should recognise that different policies are needed to tackle different problems. In addition, drug users are a mixed group of people, and what works for one may not work for another. There is no panacea in the field of illicit drugs.

The Northern Road Drug Advice Centre

The Centre has several roles in respect of illicit drugs. Most of its work involves helping opiate and amphetamine users: helping them to cope with life and helping them to reduce their drug taking. The Northern Road staff also carry out some educational and preventive work.

We said in the last chapter that the Centre was generally well-regarded among drug users. Recently, growing numbers of local opiate users seemed to be making contact with it. This increase was mainly the result of a growth in the proportion seeking help; there was evidence from several sources to suggest that the total number of local users had not risen as steeply as the number attending the Centre. The open, community-based approach has enabled Northern Road to gain the confidence of many users, and recent attempts to make the service more accessible seem to have been successful. Moreover, the moving of the detoxification unit from its setting in the psychiatric hospital two miles away into an annex of the Centre itself must have been beneficial: it will help to integrate the different parts of the Centre's work, as well as ridding the detox unit of the institutional atmosphere that some users inevitably felt before.

There is a debate about the rights and wrongs of prescribing methadone as a heroin substitute, but our research backs the view that there is no general answer to the question, and individual decisions need to be taken about individual users. Some people have been able to straighten out their lives as a result of a long period on prescribed methadone: removing the necessity to find and buy illicit opiates is for these people a real liberation. Later, when they have a commitment to their new way of life, they may be able to leave drugs behind altogether. Others are able, with the right help, to give up opiates outright, without a period of using any substitute. Others can be helped by a programme of gradual reduction.

As soon as a person has made the break and given up opiates, the problem turns to one of staying off. Many of the users impressed on us the point that it is relatively easy to give up for a short period, but the real difficulty is permanent abstinence. The Northern Road staff are aware of this, and they do spend time helping people who have given up, but there is room for more thinking about how to use the time effectively. Issues of resource allocation are partly behind the imbalance between services for those who are still users and services for ex-users: when funds are limited, the acute needs of front-line services for assisting and 'curing' addicts have a stronger case than the needs of people who have already been helped off drugs. However, money spent on detoxification and counselling to bring people off is money wasted if they later return to opiates because the follow-up services are not equally effective.

Northern Road has a particular new responsibility as a result of the AIDS threat. We have seen that many users have shared syringes in the past, and some still do. The Centre staff have been warning people about the dangers involved, and most users seem to know about the risks. Time will tell whether the recently-established needle exchange scheme will help to eradicate sharing.

The Centre does not see many users under the age of 20. This is partly a reflection of the limited scale of the heroin problem among teenagers in Portsmouth and Havant, but it is also because young users do not seek the Centre's help. Perhaps the reason is that older users tend to seek help as their troubles mount up, while young users do not perceive of their drug-taking as a problem. This is an area into which Northern Road could usefully move: to reach out to young drug users and counsel them before they make the mistakes that their elders have made. The work would be difficult and would require imagination, but its benefits would be considerable.

The local authority social services

Social workers have relatively few contacts with known drug users. When they do have clients who take illicit drugs, their role is principally to help them with other difficulties and to direct them to sources of help for the drug problem. Drug-user clients should be encouraged to go to the Northern Road Centre, and we are confident that this happens: Hampshire Social Services have a long history of involvement with drugs work, and their specialist drugs adviser is stationed at Northern Road.

Perhaps the social services have an even more important role in respect of legal drugs. Social workers see many people who abuse alcohol and many who habitually take prescribed tranquillisers. In this report we have shown that illicit drug use is strongly linked to legal drug use, particularly where there are family models of problem-oriented intoxication. Work on problems with alcohol and tranquillisers can therefore pay a second dividend by helping to reduce the likelihood that clients and other members of their families become involved with illicit drugs. The social services should as far as possible approach all drug use as a single problem area, without separating legal from illegal drugs.

The probation service

Probation officers see a substantial number of illicit drug users, many of whom have been convicted of offences involving drugs, or offences committed to obtain money for drugs. They are in a good position to counsel users about drugs and to encourage them to seek help from Northern Road. They also see ex-users and can talk over the problems that might drive them back to drugs.

With the assistance of staff from the Northern Road Centre, drop-in discussion groups for drug users have been held at probation centres, with mixed results. One group attracted a number of users on a fairly regular basis, and helped Northern Road gain a better foothold within the community; another group failed to attract users. Our impression is that the functioning group has helped the people who attend.

The probation service is clearly an important agency for helping drug users. The actual help they receive depends on the knowledge and commitment of individual probation officers, and these vary. In this subject area, the service should therefore have objectives that are clear and training that equips officers with the knowledge they need. The fact that many users pass through a period of probation should be seen as an opportunity for sustained intervention and counselling over drugs.

The police

Some people regard the police and the customs service as the agencies with the main responsibility for tackling the drugs problem. This view is based on the notion that the escalation of drug abuse can be curtailed by an efficient and tough enforcement policy: if you lock up the smugglers and the 'pushers' and crack down on ordinary users, you remove the source of supply and make it too costly (financially and legally) for people to continue taking drugs. The notion is wrong, and it leads to unrealistic expectations of the effectiveness of enforcement strategies. The experience of countries all around the world tells us that the 'war on drugs' cannot be won by force. Enormous sums of money are made in the drugs trade, and, whatever the penalties, some people are willing to take the risk. Individual users are fearful of arrest and prosecution, but the deterrent effect of the law seems to be limited: users accept that they risk trouble with the police, and many have criminal records already. It stands to reason that police and customs action puts obstacles in the way of the drugs trade and deters people from trying illicit drugs, but it would be naive to expect law enforcement to provide the main answers to the country's drug problems. Remedies have to be found that tackle the problem of demand for drugs: prevention, treatment and rehabilitation are the critical areas.

Cannabis is a real problem for the police. It makes up the largest part of the drugs trade, but causes fewest social problems. It is relatively cheap, so there is not much property crime committed to get money for it, and few people approach the drug services with cannabis addiction problems. In itself, it has little impact on users' lives when compared with other drugs. But because of the numbers of people involved, cannabis accounts for law-breaking on a far wider scale than other drugs. This puts the police in an impossible situation: on the one hand there are demands to be tough on drugs, and to pursue the thousands of people who break the law by smoking cannabis, while on the other hand there are appeals to distinguish between drug use that is damaging and drug use that is relatively harmless.

In all areas of their work the police make decisions about priorities, and the publicly-stated drugs strategy is to concentrate on hard drugs and on catching dealers. But the majority of drug arrests, both nationally and locally, are for cannabis possession. This is largely the result of the much larger numbers of people using cannabis than using any other drug. Many of the proceedings over cannabis arise from its discovery by ordinary police officers, rather than from strategic actions by the drugs squad. The predominance of cannabis proceedings also results from the fact that people involved with opiates often use cannabis too, and when searched they are found to have cannabis instead of (or as well as) hard drugs. Drug users observe the contradiction between the stated policy and the actual numbers of arrests for cannabis, and see it as an example of duplicity by the authorities.

The role of the police is largely determined by the law on drugs, but there are two ways they can help with the local efforts on treatment and prevention. The first is to ensure that arrested drug offenders are always referred to the Northern Road Centre. This could also be extended to contacts with known users who are not arrested - police officers could advise them to go along to the Centre, and give them details. The second is to place some emphasis on the under-age consumption of legal drugs. Given the connections between drinking, smoking and illicit drug taking, a campaign to stop publicans and retailers serving alcohol and tobacco to young people could be very helpful; there is no doubt, anyway, that the biggest and most dangerous drug problems facing Portsmouth and Havant are those of alcohol and tobacco, and enforcing the legal restrictions on young people's access to them should be a priority.

Teachers and those working in health education

Educational work on drugs is aimed principally at prevention. Teachers seldom come across pupils who admit illicit drug use, so they are rarely in a position to give advice and help to users. It is important, therefore, that teachers know about the Northern Road Centre so that in these rare cases they know where to turn for advice and where to refer the user.

Preventive educational work should be approached carefully. Few school pupils try illicit drugs, and even fewer go further than experimentation. Our survey suggests that an approach to drugs education that enhances the image of drugs as glamorous, adventurous or rebellious is likely to make some pupils more interested in them. It would be a tragedy if, with the best intentions, teachers or others who work with young people actually made matters worse. Those who wish to tackle the subject should do so in collaboration with the county Health Education service, which has adopted a sensitive approach to drugs as part of a 'life-skills' perspective on young people's problems, rather than as a subject in its own right. Above all, people working with teenagers should note that alcohol and tobacco are their most important drug problems, and should not be mesmerised by the sensational publicity around the use of illicit drugs: there is not a drugs epidemic in Portsmouth and Havant.

General practitioners

General practitioners are an important source of help for users of illicit drugs. A recent study by Glanz and Taylor estimated that there are 9,500 consultations with GPs for opiate misuse in England and Wales every four weeks; it also estimated that each year there are 138 consultations for opiate misuse for every 100 GPs in the Wessex health region, which includes Portsmouth and Havant. The load is unlikely to be spread evenly between doctors: some will average less than one opiate user a year, while others, in areas where the drugs scene is more active, will see a number of users more than once.

The Northern Road Centre receives many referrals from GPs. This shows that GPs generally respond positively to requests for help from users. However, we heard complaints from users that some GPs are not sympathetic, and want little to do with patients who have drug problems: they said that addicts are treated as pests and as potential sources of trouble. All GPs should be reminded that they can play an important role in helping drug users, and should be encouraged to make referrals to Northern Road. There is another problem in that a few GPs seem to be an 'easy touch' for drug users seeking prescriptions for opiates (especially Diconal) and tranquillisers, and these drugs do find their way onto the illicit market. While doctors need to deal sympathetically with drug misusers, they also need to take care when prescribing psychoactive drugs.

Monitoring illicit drug use

Regular monitoring of the level and character of drug abuse within different areas of the county is important: the response of services can be appropriate only if there is data on the scale of the problems. This is true both for those helping users and for those trying to prevent further growth of the problem.

Probation officers are a good source of information. Although they only see a small proportion of drug users in a locality, they are in a good position to provide information on trends. Even a simple head-count of user clients will give helpful trend data over time. Although social workers see even fewer illicit drug users, the same data collection by the social services will give additional information: there is little overlap between the drug users known to the two services. Senior officers in the probation service and social services are less aware of what is happening on the ground in respect of drugs than are the people working under them. The seniors, on the other hand, can play a vital role in ensuring that any local monitoring is actually carried through. Social workers and probation officers are busy and they tend to give extra form-filling a low priority.

Most research has shown that local GP surveys are not good sources of information about drug users. The response rates are usually low, probably because many GPs see few users, and because doctors have a large postbag and questionnaires do not get top priority. Doctors already have a duty to notify the Home Office about opiate addicts they treat. The postal survey by Glanz and Taylor did achieve a good response rate, however, with 72 per cent of sampled GPs replying.

Police records and chemists' records are good sources of trend data. However, there are severe problems of confidentiality. The sort of data made available to PSI for this one-off study is probably unobtainable in its raw form for on-going monitoring. A summary and digest of the information could be produced by the officers who already handle the information, and this would preserve confidentiality.

Monitoring of the number of user contacts with drug advice centres and other drug workers is currently being organised under the aegis of the Wessex Regional Health Authority. This work needs to be integrated into any other local or county monitoring arrangements. Local monitoring meetings of professionals active in the drugs field could be very useful. Ideally they should involve people working at client level, although it is hard to see how so many people in an area could be brought together effectively. Perhaps a two-tier system would work, whereby meetings within agencies pass on information via representatives to inter-agency meetings. As a minimum, the local drugs advisory committees should have a twice-yearly agenda item specifically devoted to a discussion of any changes in the prevalence of local drug use.

A national problem seen on a local scale

This report has examined the illicit use of drugs in one geographical area, and our comments about services are therefore directed principally to the people working there. We hope, however, that the value of the study extends beyond the boundaries of Portsmouth and Havant. The aim of the project has been to place the national drugs problem in a local context, but not to take a parochial view, because many of the issues tackled in Hampshire are the same ones facing services throughout the country. Many of the points made here about prevention, enforcement and care will be relevant to the concerns of professionals elsewhere in Britain. The problem may be a national one, but it manifests itself in ways that are most clearly seen with a local perspective.

Drug abuse can be tackled effectively only if the facts are understood - not only by the agencies that have contact with illicit drug users, but also by the general public. Stereotypes and mythology have to be left behind, along with the notion that there are easy solutions. Above all, a sensible and honest approach should acknowledge that many of us use drugs (legal drugs for the most part) to change the way we feel, and that illicit drugs make up only one aspect of drug abuse. Strategies for prevention and recovery need to take into account the fact that the illegal drugs problem exists within a social framework of approved drug-taking. The approach may be uncomfortable, but it is the only one that offers hope for stemming the growth of this otherwise baffling, self-destructive behaviour.

REFERENCES

Alan Glanz, Colin Taylor, 'Findings of a national survey of the role of general practitioners in the treatment of opiate abuse: extent of contact with opiate misusers', *British Medical Journal*, Vol 293, 16 August 1986, pp427-430.

Richard Hartnoll, Emmanuelle Daviaud, Roger Lewis, Martin Mitcheson, *Drug Problems: Assessing Local Needs*, (London, Drug Indicators Project, Birkbeck College, University of London, 1985).

Alan Marsh, Joy Dobbs, Amanda White, *Adolescent Drinking*, (London, HMSO, 1986).

Joy Mott, 'Self-Reported Cannabis Use in Great Britain in 1981', *British Journal of Addiction* 80, 1985, pp37-43.

Martin Plant, David Peck, Elaine Samuel, *Alcohol, Drugs and School-leavers*, (London, Tavistock, 1985).

Jackie Powell, Robin Lovelock, *Northern Road: a study of developing services for drug misusers*, Social Services Research and Intelligence Unit Report No. 16, (Portsmouth, SSRIU, 1987).

Colin Pritchard, Mary Fielding, N. Choudry, Malcolm Cox and Ian Diamond, 'Incidence of Drug and Solvent Use in 'Normal' Fourth and Fifth Year Comprehensive School Children - some Socio-behavioural Characteristics', *British Journal of Social Work* 16, 1986, pp341-351.

Cindy Prowse, *Drugs and Substance Abuse: An Investigation by Self Report Questionnaire of Fourthformers in Three Schools in Three Different Areas*, (unpublished MSc dissertation, 1985).

Andrew Tyler, *Street Drugs*, (London, New English Library, 1986).

APPENDIX:

Example of the schools questionnaire

This is a copy of the questionnaire form completed by third, fourth and fifth year pupils in secondary schools. The forms filled in by younger and older pupils were amended to account for the age differences, but were very similar to the one shown here.

Survey of School Pupils' Views

DO NOT WRITE YOUR NAME ANYWHERE ON THIS FORM

WHEN YOU HAVE FILLED IN THE FORM
PLEASE SEAL IT IN THE ENVELOPE

All the answers you give will be treated confidentially. This is an anonymous survey - that means there is no name on the form and no one will be able to tell who filled it in. Teachers will not see any of the forms. Please answer the questions by ticking the boxes which apply to you.

1. **Are you a boy or a girl?**

I am a boy ☐

I am a girl ☐

---

2. **How old are you?**

____

---

3. **Which of these areas do you live in?**

DO NOT GIVE YOUR FULL ADDRESS

Cosham	☐	Waterlooville/Purbrook/Cowplain	☐
North End (Stamshaw, Tipner, Hilsea)	☐	Leigh Park	☐
Central Portsmouth (Kingston, Milton, Fratton, Copnor, Buckland, Portsea)	☐	Havant Town	☐
Southsea	☐	Hayling Island	☐
Paulsgrove/Wymering	☐	Other	☐
Drayton/Farlington	☐		

Look at the map we have given you, if you need an idea of these areas

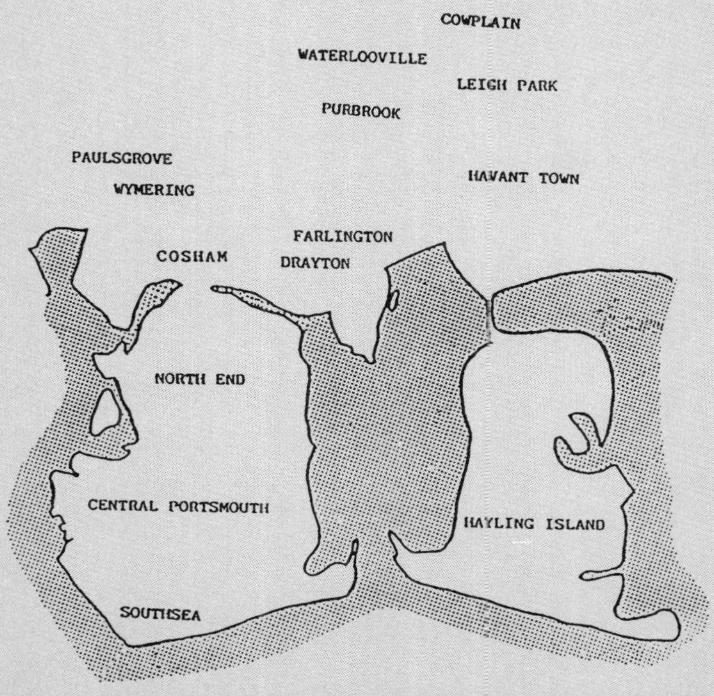

4. **Does your father have a job?**

No, he doesn't have a job ☐

Yes, he has a job ☐

Please describe the sort of work he does

____

____

And does your mother have a job?

No, she doesn't have a job ☐

Yes, she has a job ☐

Please describe the sort of work she does

____

____

---

5. **If you discuss the following subjects with your parents, do you usually agree or disagree?**

	Always Agree	Mostly Agree	Mostly Disagree	Always Disagree	We Never Discuss This
School					
Your friends					
Politics/The News					
Boyfriends/Girlfriends					
Leaving school/jobs					
Religion					
The way you spend money					
Your hobbies					
The time you come home					

6. Do you get pocket money from your family?

No ☐ Yes ☐

IF YES - How much do you get each week? ______________

Do you earn money yourself?

No ☐ Yes ☐

IF YES - How much do you earn each week? ______________

---

7. Did you do any of the following things <u>outside school</u> in the past <u>seven</u> days?

Please tick the boxes that apply

Watch TV at home ☐

Play a musical instrument ☐

Listen to records or tapes ☐

Go out with the rest of your family ☐

Read a book ☐

Go to a party ☐

Play sports or go swimming ☐

Do voluntary work with people (for example, visiting the elderly) ☐

Play chess, draughts, cards or other board games ☐

Listen to the radio ☐

Go to a pub ☐

Watch a rented video ☐

Go to a youth club, guides, scouts or similar youth group ☐

Mend or work on a bicycle, motorbike or car ☐

Draw or paint ☐

Go to church, Sunday school or other religious classes ☐

Go to the cinema or theatre ☐

8. **In the last two weeks, have you read...**

...a magazine or comic? Yes ☐ No ☐

...a music paper? Yes ☐ No ☐

...a newspaper? Yes ☐ No ☐

IF YES, what are they called ____________________

____

____

---

9. **What are your <u>three</u> favourite TV programmes?**

____

____

____

---

10. **Think of the last time you went out in the evening <u>without</u> your parents - for example, to a club, disco, film or to meet friends. What time did your parents tell you to come home?**

____

The next six questions are about cigarettes, alcoholic drinks and other things that alter the way you feel.

Remember that no one will know who filled in the form. Please help us by giving honest and truthful answers.

11. **Most people know someone who smokes cigarettes. What about you - have you ever tried smoking cigarettes?**

No ☐ Yes ☐

IF YES - Have you smoked a cigarette in the last week? No ☐ Yes ☐

...in the last month? No ☐ Yes ☐

12. Most people know someone who drinks alcohol (beer, wine, gin and so on). What about you - have you ever tried an alcoholic drink?

No ☐ Yes ☐

IF YES - Have you had an alcoholic drink in the last week? No ☐ Yes ☐
...in the last month? No ☐ Yes ☐

---

13. Do you know anyone who has sniffed glue, or sniffed other substances?

No ☐ Yes ☐

Have you ever sniffed glue or other substances?

No ☐ Yes ☐

IF YES - Have you done this in the last week? No ☐ Yes ☐
...in the last month? No ☐ Yes ☐

---

14. Do you know anyone who has smoked cannabis ('dope', 'blow', 'black', 'hash', 'grass' and marijuana)?

No ☐ Yes ☐

Have you ever smoked cannabis yourself?

No ☐ Yes ☐

IF YES - Have you had any in the last week? No ☐ Yes ☐
...in the last month? No ☐ Yes ☐

---

15. Do you know anyone who has taken heroin ('skag' or 'smack')?

No ☐ Yes ☐

Have you ever taken heroin yourself?

No ☐ Yes ☐

IF YES - Have you had any in the last week? No ☐ Yes ☐
...in the last month? No ☐ Yes ☐

16. Do you know anyone who has taken amphetamine tablets or powder ('speed')?

No ☐ Yes ☐

Have you ever taken amphetamines yourself?

No Yes

IF YES - Have you had any in the last week? No ☐ Yes ☐
...in the last month? No ☐ Yes ☐

---

17. Do you know anyone who has taken any other drug?

No ☐ Yes ☐

IF YES - What drug is that? ______________________

Have you ever tried any other drug?

No ☐ Yes ☐

IF YES - What drug is that? ______________________

Have you had any in the last week? No ☐ Yes ☐
...in the last month? No ☐ Yes ☐

---

18. Would you ever do any of these things? Please tick the boxes if you think you would.

Get involved in a fight ☐

Ride on a motorbike without a helmet ☐

Go pot-holing, mountaineering or hang-gliding ☐

Play cards for money ☐

Drive a car without a licence ☐

Accept a lift from a stranger ☐

Play truant ☐

Write or spray graffiti on a wall ☐

Steal something ☐

19. **Think about what will happen when you leave school. Put ticks in the boxes to describe how you feel.**

	Very Good	Good	Fair	Poor	Very Poor
My chances of getting the qualifications I want are...					
My chances of getting a job are...					
My chances of getting an interesting job are...					

THANK YOU FOR YOUR HELP